Secrets, Lies, Silence

JOHN T. SKINNER

ISBN-13: 978-1-9999090-0-0

DEDICATION

To my family: Linda, Jayne, Sara, Sadie and Benjamin.
Battered, bruised but never bitter.

"When they thought we had gone to hell,
We came right back and rang our bell."
Adapted from Thomas Merton's poem 'All the Way Down' (1980)

CONTENTS

ACKNOWLEDGEMENTS

Writing this book was an emotional rollercoaster. It sent my blood pressure, normally low, ridiculously high. My wife Linda, who was with me every step of the way, had various stress-related physical complaints. Without her support and partnership in this venture, this book would never have been finished. To my daughter Jayne Morris who motivated me to complete the project and helped edit the book. Thanks Jayne for reliving some of the traumas with us. To my first readers whose constructive criticism and support gave shape to the final content of the book: thanks to Jayne Morris, Linda Skinner, Syd Niven, Michael Connaughton, George Elerick and Danielle Hinton. Finally, my daughter Sadie who proofread the book, often through a veil of misty tears. Thank you, Sadie.

PREFACE

To be abused, is to be caught in a vicious cycle of secrets, lies and silence. Abuse must be kept secret. It must be hidden and remain in the dark. If the secret is in danger of being revealed, then the lies increase. Malicious lies. More abuse. The worst of all is the silence. People you thought would stand up, be outraged and demand justice, remain silent. Even when the secret is out, the lies exposed and the truth is staring them in the face, they choose to remain in the secret and lies. They don't want their world upset, to become insecure or isolated. The silence magnifies the abuse.

Abuse comes from many sources: family and friends, professional institutions, church and charity. Abuse comes in many disguises: physical, sexual, emotional, institutional, ideological. Whatever the form, the outcome is the same: secrets, lies and silence. When you are abused, your life is put on hold, your history is stolen from you. Only when the secret is out, the lies exposed, do you then get your history back and the opportunity to heal, to move forward.

The people named in this book were given numerous opportunities to put things right. All chose to remain in the secrets, lies and silence. My hope in exposing their abuse and bringing it into the open is that they take the opportunity to redeem the past.

FOREWORD

Visionaries are a peculiar breed. A rare mix of passion and pragmatism, of leadership and apparent lunacy as they think the unthinkable and venture forth, often without the detail and clarity many crave before stepping out. Valiant yet vulnerable they frequently risk rejection and resource issues while others prefer comfort and the certainty of the familiar. They are individuals, rich in complexity and seeming contradictions. Though they can make many nervous they can often be fascinating, attractive and graced with the ability to draw people together and to make remarkable things happen. John Skinner is such a character.

Many years ago, I heard this:
"One step ahead you're a leader. Two steps ahead you're a pioneer. Three steps ahead, you're a martyr!"

The challenge for any visionary is to lead people beyond their fears without people wanting to kill them before the future is realised. Most, of course, are reluctant to admit the presence of murderous thoughts within. John Skinner has certainly not been a stranger to dealing with the dark side of the human condition, either within himself or within others. Most of us could not have imagined so much trauma and difficulty being packed into one life. Rejection and betrayal are at their most deadly when carried out by those who claim to be close!

I first met John Skinner in his Whittingham phase and have been privileged to call him "friend" ever since. With him on the same day the vision for The House that John Built was born, walking through times of adventure and of uncertainty, financial risk and the founding of the motherhouse of the Northumbria Community – and the beginnings of the other end of The House that John Built in Turkey – I've seen the triumphs and the tragedies up close! I've sat with John in some of his darkest times of broken health & promises, relational ruptures as well as the frustrations of his future hopes and dreams. The impact on his family can probably never be fully told. John's story deserves to be!

"I want my history back" is certainly not about creating a happy memory box. What is contained in these pages is not an easy read. Full of honesty and humanity, they contain information which will shock some and stir reactions. I've heard other narratives of judgement and blame yet few have genuinely enquired about what has happened. Perhaps it is just too easy to accept a handed down narrative than face the consequences of establishing truth and justice!

My hope is the following pages may stir some questions:
- about the abuse of power and position
- about the rhetoric of courage spoken by the comfortable
- about the value of relationships over reputation
- about our own willingness to face difficulty with a real determination to be different

.... and about the spirit that does not quit in the face of adversity but perseveres, and even continues to explore new territories and ideas that may lead us and others into a better tomorrow.

At its heart, this book contains a quest for truth and justice and our responses will reveal something of ourselves. Passivity or indifference are not real options once we know. Without truth and justice, we each live at the mercy of ill-intention and join with the ongoing protection of those who abuse, so their work can continue. My hope is that, through the reading of these pages, we also may play our part in the quest. **Syd Niven, October 2017**

"The peace demanded by God has two boundaries: first, the truth; second, justice. A community of peace can exist only when it does not rest on a lie or on injustice. Wherever a community of peace endangers or suffocates truth and justice, the community of peace must be broken and the battle must be declared. If the battle from both sides is really about truth and justice, then the community of peace, even when externally broken, will be realised more deeply and strongly in the battle for this very cause..." (Bonhoeffer, 'On the theological foundation of the work of the World Alliance' in Ecumenical, Academic and Pastoral Work 1931-1932, p.365).

INTRODUCTION: DEAD MAN WALKING

There I was on an operating table in a Turkish hospital, in 2016, in the middle of a heart attack with the cardiologist telling me in broken English that if he did not sort me out immediately, then I would be dead within the hour. He also added, "I will probably kill you doing this, but it's the last chance you have. You're a dead man walking. What do you want me to do?"

Two years earlier, I had an angina attack while visiting the UK. It was on Christmas Day, in 2014, and started early in the afternoon. The pain came and went all day as I overdosed myself on nitro-glycerine. As soon as my grandchildren went to bed, I phoned for an ambulance and headed to the nearest Accident and Emergency (A&E) department.

I was already familiar with the procedures. In 1998-9, I had had a series of heart attacks each one ending up with a visit to A&E, followed by time spent in intensive care or on an acute ward. Then you wait, your family waits and your friends wait to see if you die or get sent home. I discovered that when you are ill, you do a lot of waiting around and thinking. Finally, in 1999, on my 44th birthday, I had a quadruple bypass. It took place on the same date, at nearly the same time my father died. He was also 44. A bit spooky really. He had had a massive heart attack.

In 2014, they gave me an aspirin, a blood-thinning injection and then booked me in for an angiogram to see what was happening in my coronary arteries. The results made depressing news: my arteries were pretty much blocked again and the British cardiologist said there were no more operations or procedures they could do if I were to have another heart incident. I was sent home with a death sentence.

Back to 2016. The Turkish cardiologist grew impatient waiting for an answer. He wanted to get started. In my own mind, I had already resigned myself to dying, said goodbye to my family, sorted my affairs and was ready to accept my fate. "What the hell, there's nothing to lose," I thought to myself. As soon as I said "yes," the whole of his team jumped into action and I was surrounded by a green army, wearing very colourful bandanas.

The cardiologist turned out to be the Elvis Presley of angiograms. Basically, he put a wire into an artery in my groin, then pushed it up towards my heart where he could gain access to my coronary arteries. He then looked for spaces where he could insert a tiny balloon, which is then inflated and a stent (small tube) is added. The purpose of both stent and balloon is to try and widen the blocked artery to get the blood flowing again. The doctor then turned into Elvis and literally did *shake*, *rattle* and *roll* throughout the whole procedure, orchestrating his team with exaggerated hand movements. Unaware that I knew some Turkish, he went through a whole vocabulary of expletives and a range of emotions, including despair, frustration and anxiety. I was fully conscious through it all, watching the monitor above my head showing the doctor's dexterity as he carefully negotiated my arteries.

After inflating several balloons and adding two stents, he declared it was all over. However, there was one small problem: I still had acute chest pain. When he looked back at the monitor, I could see the panic in his face. One of the arteries he had stented had stopped flowing. I discovered later that this artery is nicknamed "the widow maker" because when blocked, it is notorious for causing fatal heart attacks.

The next few minutes were intense. Dr Elvis was sweating profusely and shouting expletives at g-d, the team and me. Then the tension broke. There were high fives all around, the team were genuinely excited and everyone relaxed. I looked up at the screen, blood was now flowing through the widow maker. I would be returning from the dead, back to my wife. Dr Elvis had saved me, not killed me.

They say that when you are dying, your whole life passes before your eyes. As Dr Elvis did his thing, I suddenly became aware that the most traumatic events I had experienced in my life were demanding my attention. I was shocked that these events would be the last things I would get to think about if all of this went wrong. There were four of them and they presented themselves in chronological order, starting with the earliest and the most traumatic of them all. I think my mind had insisted on placing them in an orderly queue as a condition of allowing them back into consciousness. I was rather surprised that looking at them again (something I prefer not to do) had not evoked the usual range of overwhelming emotions that I find exhausting and nauseating. These had been traumatic and abusive events visited upon myself, my wife Linda and our kids by my church, my community, and friends, all of whom we not only trusted but had invested our lives in.

At the very front of the queue was an event relating to my mother. Some years earlier, I had discovered her deadly secret which provided answers as to why I had had such a disturbed childhood and why that secret had haunted me most of my adult life. I was not sure why any of these traumas had turned up at all since there was absolutely nothing I could do or say to respond to them. Still thinking I was about to die, I resigned myself to the fact that those who had caused myself and my family so much anguish would never be held accountable for what they had done. More upsetting was the knowledge that our story would never be told and anything meaningful found in it would be lost forever.

Fast forward to today. It's 2017 and I am sitting in my study looking across the bay to the Holy Island of Lindisfarne in Northumberland. Recently, I had to visit a psychiatrist in Belfast to have a mental health assessment relating to traumatic event number two. She wanted to know my whole story and question after question followed as she dug deeper into my psyche. At the end of it, we were both emotionally exhausted. Linda said the psychiatrist had been composed when she went into the session, but looked shell-shocked when she came out. I, too, was recovering from the emotional roller coaster. At the end of our session she asked me a very simple question: "Why do you feel sorry for the people who abuse you?" Writing this book is my attempt to answer that question. She also suggested that I might benefit from some further therapy and said I should find a suitable therapist in the UK as soon as possible.

I have had therapy several times and am thankful to those who emotionally invested in listening to my story. I decided that if it really was time to tell my story, I needed to do it for myself because I need the therapy again. I think talking to one person would not make a difference, but speaking to a wider audience through my writing would. I plan to write my story as a series of psychoanalytical events. As a result, each of the four traumatic events will act as a reference point from which the narrative will emerge. I hope you find something meaningful as I tell you how I tried and succeeded in not letting these traumas define my life, but rather to re-define it, opening a new chapter in my life each time.

1. A TOXIC BELIEF

I held my breath as the heavy metal door closed behind me. The sound of the bolts sliding across to lock it echoed in my mind and signalled my loss of freedom. I was on the secure lock-up ward at Cherry Knowle Hospital, formerly known as the Sunderland Borough Lunatic Asylum. I was seventeen years old.

My crime? I had made several suicide attempts, including jumping off a motorway bridge. I didn't know how to handle the grief of losing three of the most important people in my life. I also self-medicated with alcohol which had become my trusted friend since I was fourteen years old.

The asylum had been built in Victorian times and, looking at the ward, nothing much had changed even after it had been rebranded as a hospital. The ward was an open sitting/dining room. There were several dining tables, in military order, and a series of armchairs dotted here and there.

The scariest part? My fellow inmates. A few of them looked alien-like with greyish, purple faces, which I later discovered was the result of the long-term use of the drug Largactil. Largactil was also behind "the ward shuffle" as the same patients would walk around the room, making short, sliding steps with their feet barely leaving the floor. Little did I know that, in the space of an hour, I would be having my first Largactil experience.

I spotted out of the corner of my eye a man who would be my neighbour in the communal dormitory. He was sitting in a chair, rocking back and forwards and staring into space, muttering to himself. Apparently, he did this every day and as I discovered for myself, every night. Two other patients were standing in the room, both engrossed in conversations, not with each other, but with themselves. The only person who appeared to be normal was a young man sitting in a corner, smoking cigarettes. I made a mental note to seek him out later.

The charge nurse and his assistant ushered me into their office. I was welcomed by a verbal assault, labelling me as "weak" and as someone who needed "to man up". When I reacted, they both grabbed me and I was frog-marched to what had once been a padded cell. It was white tiled, cold and intimidating. They ordered me to remove my clothes. When I refused, they aggressively stripped me naked and I was then forced onto the mattress on the cell floor, face down. I felt the injections going into my buttocks. The smell from one of them was gross, the dreaded Largactil! I started to feel woozy immediately. The nurses threw a dressing gown over me and left the room. I just managed to turn over onto my back before a deep paralysis set in. I couldn't move. When my family visited later in the day, I still couldn't move and my speech was slurred. When they complained, the charge nurse informed them I had been sectioned for 28 days. During that time, I was under his supervision and there was no way out.

The next day, the effects of the drugs had worn off. I could wear pyjamas and a dressing gown and was readmitted to the ward. It was still a scary place. Who do you talk to when most people are talking to themselves? I headed for the lad in the corner, still smoking cigarettes. His name was Jonnie, he was an alcoholic and had been admitted during a bout of 'delirium tremens' which are caused by withdrawal from alcohol. By the sounds of it, he had arrived on the ward in a bad way. For the first three days he was confused, hearing voices, shaking uncontrollably and had several fits. This condition is extremely dangerous and can kill you. I could tell from his body language and the tone of his voice that he had now sunk into the deep depression that often occurs after such an attack. I had found a friend, but I realised his depression meant I needed to be careful not to invade his space.

Jonnie gave me the low-down on both staff and patients and, occasionally, his satirical side would kick in. He could be extremely funny. Paul, the charge nurse, was a born-again Christian. "O my g-d," I shuddered when he told me that and anticipated dark times ahead. He was also a military man and ran the ward like a military operation, which explains the symmetry of the dining tables. His presence dominated the ward and the other staff were pretty much extensions of his will.

Jonnie knew little about the patients. At most, as I had observed, they were locked in their own worlds. The man who rocked all day and night was called Paddy. He was a paranoid schizophrenic and was heavily sedated because of bouts of violence. Jonnie had witnessed Paddy flip his lid twice; both times the nurses were the target. He was a small and wiry man, but muscular and fit. Strangely, the only time he would take a break from rocking, was when he went off to engage in sexual activity with his boyfriend who was nicknamed "Big Mike". Mike was a seriously big man.

He was obviously in the wrong place as he had special needs, not a mental health condition. He had the mental age of an eight-year-old trapped in the body of a sumo wrestler. He had been on this ward for years, as had most patients.

My conversation with Jonnie was disturbed when the born-again, military man appeared on the ward. It was time to do the daily exercise routine. We were placed in a line, one behind the other. When the music started, so did "the ward shuffle". We shuffled around the room, barely moving from the spot, like some strange lunatic asylum conga. I was desperate to laugh, but I knew I would experience the wrath of Paul, the born-again, military man. I comforted myself with the knowledge that because I recognised the irony of it all, I still had my sanity. The ward had a very strict routine and woe betide anyone who messed it up!

After the lunatic asylum conga, I was assigned to the team who set the tables for lunch. I was rather disturbed to discover that the knives, forks and spoons were made of metal. My fellow table-setter was part of the purple-faced and ward-shuffle fraternity. He would shuffle around the table, then stop and stare at me. He had small, piggy type eyes that were black and complimented his purple face and what appeared to be a jet-black toupee, which was slightly tilted to one side. He had this weird and uncanny laugh that would accompany the staring, which made me uneasy. As we finished the final setting, he grabbed a knife and lunged across the table at me. As a ward shuffler, I was surprised at how nimble he became in that moment. I just managed to jump backwards, out of harm's way. One of the nurses saw the incident and came across to tell me that the whole thing was harmless and I needn't worry about it. Harry did this to all the new boys; it was his way of having fun. I wasn't convinced. If I hadn't jumped backwards, I would have had a knife in my belly. Unfortunately, the worst was yet to come.

My first night had been spent on the floor of the former padded cell. It was cold, but the drugs did their job and I slept in relative safety. As evening approached on the second day, I dreaded the new sleeping arrangements. Bedtime was at 9pm, with lights out at 9.30pm sharp (military timetable). The dormitory had a cold ceramic floor and the steel-framed beds were arranged either side of the room with the same military precision as the dining tables. I was assigned to a bed that had "Psycho Paddy" (the rocker) at one side and "Big Mike" (the eight-year-old sumo wrestler) at the other. It was a nightmare and I didn't anticipate getting very much sleep. One consolation was that Harry, the purple faced ward shuffler who had tried to stab me, was at the far side of the room on the opposite side so I could keep an eye on him if he decided on any other dangerous pranks. I slid into my metal bed, propped the pillows up so I could get an all-round view of the room and pulled the sheets right up to my chin. The lights were dimmed at 9.30pm, filling the room with eerie shadows. How the hell did I end up here? Big Mike (the eight-year-old sumo wrestler) soon fell into a deep sleep, punctuated by snoring and loud farting; his toxic wind filling the room. Soon the whole room came alive with the nocturnal chorus of the secure ward choir of Sunderland Borough Lunatic Asylum.

At about 4am, I reluctantly took a break from my surveillance and went to the loo. Standing at the communal latrine, having a pee, I suddenly became aware that somebody was standing behind me. I turned around and there was Big Mike in his string vest and nothing else. It was obvious by the size of his horse-like-willie that he had sex on his mind and I was the object of his desire. He leant over to kiss me and I pushed him away as hard as I could. He fell backwards onto his bottom. He was soon up on his feet again, his huge horse-like-willie swaying menacingly as he moved in for a second attempt. I jumped up and punched him as hard as I could in the face. His nose popped and started running with blood. Big Mike, who could easily tear me apart limb by limb, looked at me as a child would when they have been harmed. He then looked at his vest, which had turned red from his popped and bleeding nose, and burst into tears. His huge horse-like-willie began to retreat and soon became the size of an eight-year-old boy's finger. Big Mike then threw himself on the floor, assumed the foetal position and sobbed like a baby. The night nurse arrived and I was sent back to bed while Big Mike was cleaned up and taken to another ward for treatment.

The rising bell went at 6.30am and before I could get out of bed, the born-again, military man took my arm and pulled me up and into his office. He slapped my face and announced he would have no violence on his ward. His assistant arrived and I was frog-marched again to the former padded cell. I took my own clothes off, laid face down on the mattress, had the injections, quickly turned over on my back and waited for the arrival of the paralysis. At least I would be out of it for the rest of the day. I got to spend three weeks on the lock-up ward. Both Jonnie and I kept our noses clean, followed all the routines, took part in the daily lunatic asylum conga and said, "Yes Sir, no Sir" to the born-again, military man who could be controlled by stroking his ego. There were no further incidents and I was transferred to an open ward for my last week.

This proved to be more traumatic in an unexpected way. On the lock-up ward, the inmates (other than Jonnie) had lost the battle for their sanity years earlier. On the open and mixed ward, the battle was raging as the patients fought depression, anxiety, psychosis and addiction. I became the confidant for many people and found that sharing my own struggle to survive was strangely comforting and hopefully helpful to others.

I left Cherry Knowle Hospital (Sunderland Borough Lunatic Asylum) battered and bruised and more vulnerable than when I was first admitted. The psychiatrist's logic for admitting me to the lock-up ward was a form of shock treatment that inferred that any more suicide attempts would be met with further lock up in the asylum. I guess it worked because I never made any suicide attempt again. When the demons returned with a vengeance, I teamed up with my best friend alcohol, affectionately nicknamed "DD" (Dreaded Drink). We started hanging out together more frequently and eventually became inseparable for a while.

To explain to you how I ended up in a lock-up ward in an old lunatic asylum, then I must ask you to join me as I revisit my childhood and the place where I was brought up. I do not intend to bore you with a lot of details, but want to draw your attention to the people and events that shaped my life prior to my asylum experience. The most relevant details are that I grew up in two homes, two families, and with two mothers, which were the source of a lot of conflict.

Let me introduce you to Jarrow, the place where I was born and raised and to my first home and family. Jarrow is in the north of England, on the banks of the River Tyne, famous for its shipbuilding industry since 1852. We built every kind of ship, including merchant and warships so that in the First and Second World Wars we were a target for enemy fighters. Jarrow was a hard town, traditionally patriarchal and conservative with a small 'c'. Men worked hard in the yards and played hard down the pub. Women knew their place yet were the real matriarchs, controlling the weekly pay packet, out of which they gave their husbands pocket money to spend on beer and cigarettes. We were working class and very proud of it.

My first home and family were my nana (grandmother) and granda (grandfather). Both my mam and dad had to work long hours to make ends meet, so from a baby to around the age of eleven, I spent a great deal of time at my nana and granda's. My granda, Timothy Proctor, worked in shipbuilding all his life. He served his apprenticeship as a boiler maker and went on to become a master boilermaker, the highest accolade in his trade. Tim was a short, stocky man with hands like shovels and a great bulbous nose, which I am glad I never inherited. He had a fiery temper that mellowed with age, though he was always ready for a fight after a couple of brandies.

My enduring memory of Granda was going to meet him off the bus when he returned from work. He wore the compulsory Geordie flat cap with moleskin breeks (trousers), a wool weskit (waistcoat) with a silver pocket watch chain dangling across the front of it. His leather gallusses (braces) sat on his collarless shirt and, to finish it off, there was his black donkey jacket and black leather steel-toe boots. His tea (up North we call the evening meal "tea" and lunch "dinner") had to be on the table by the time he had taken off his jacket and cap, not a moment sooner or later. I would then sit on his knee as he ate his meat and potatoes, mostly using a knife. He smelled of the shipyard: of oil, grease, smoke and iron.

My nana, Ada, was the sweetest, kindest woman you could meet. She was small and thin with grey hair tied into a bun. She had a wrinkled face from hard work, stress and smoking too much. Nana was the peacekeeper in the family and she knew how to keep Granda on a lead when his temper got the better of him. Nana was required to pay all the bills, shop for food, prepare all the meals, clothe the kids, save a little and help any neighbours who had fallen on hard times.

My first school was five minutes from their house so until I was eleven and went to the big school, I spent most of my time with them. Dad would drop me off on a morning and pick me up at night. Nana and Granda represented security for me. There was order and a routine in the house. Meals were on time, at the same time every day. Nana started the day early so she could scrub her front door step and then get breakfast ready. There were days for shopping, washing, ironing, cleaning, and visiting friends and neighbours.

They lived in a close-knit community in a three-bed semi-detached house with a lounge, a dining room and a fair-sized kitchen. Built before World War II, it had a V sign written on the wall next to the front door not only celebrating the Allied Victory, but also the fact the house had survived the bombing. The two big gardens at the front and back of the house were immaculate. At the back, Granda had a shed for his tools and a greenhouse that always had the aroma of fresh tomatoes. The back garden was given over to growing vegetables (as it had throughout the war) and were a significant part of the household diet. The lawns at the front of the house were rich green and the plant beds were full of roses; only roses because Granda loved them.

Their four children had left the nest many years ago, all except my auntie Freda. When she was four years old, a teenage boy deliberately picked her up and dropped her upside down onto her head. As a result, she suffered brain damage and while in hospital was exposed to polio, an infectious disease that causes paralysis. The combination of the brain damage and polio led to a rapid deterioration in her physical condition. Within two years, she could not walk and required a wheelchair. Then all her limbs became bent and buckled, her hands especially. Disability was hidden in those days because of prejudice and superstition. Nana and Granda would have none of that and brought up Auntie Freda to be a fearlessly independent woman who would go on to marry and set up her own home. Nana and Granda's house represented family, security, stability, order and freedom from anxiety.

When I was eleven and due to go to the big school, home and family shifted back to my mam and dad. Life at home with my other family - Mam, Dad, older sister Freda and older brother Alan - was insecure, unstable, chaotic and anxiety producing. My parents were both incredible grafters (workers). Dad had been discharged from the Navy after the war with no transferable skills. He met my mam when his ship docked at Granda's shipyard and was brought home for tea. He tried his hand at various jobs from milkman to bus driver, clerk and machinist. Mam was a qualified hairdresser and had been offered a job in Paris before she got married. She ended up in a backstreet hairdressing shop, in nearby Hebburn, working for a family friend. She started with osteoarthritis in her early thirties, which unusually in her case, attacked all her joints. Basically, it's a disease of the cartilage, a soft material that acts as a buffer between your joints and prevents friction. Over a period of ten years, all her joints were effected and some began to breakdown as bone on bone rubbed together causing them to splinter. All that time she kept working, getting taxis to work because she couldn't walk, then standing on her feet, sometimes for twelve-hour shifts. I never once heard her complain about her illness, nor the acute pain that went with it.

My dad was from Kent and the family myth was that his dad had eloped with my nana Daisy and as a result was disinherited and cut off from his wealthy family. Nana Daisy was said to have been from a tinker or travelling family. Not sure if that is true or not, one incident suggests it may well have been. When I was nine years old, we went on holiday for the first and last time. Nana Daisy was given the job of looking after my rabbit Twitch. When my dad went to pick him up, Nana announced she had boiled Twitch in a pot and ate him in a stew. She said it was ridiculous to have a rabbit for a pet. I was gutted. She was a tough cookie who smoked woodbine cigarettes with one continually hanging out the side of her mouth and drank endless cups of strong, brown tea, laced with sugar and sickly sweet condensed milk.

Dad rarely talked about his family. One story I can remember was when his mam chased him down the street with a knife, threatening to cut his ear off for being cheeky. The other was the day his dad died when he was just ten years old. That probably explains why dad was emotionally withdrawn. He found it difficult to show affection and would tighten up if you tried to give him a hug. He had a sharp temper but his bark was worse than his bite, unlike "Mother". He read cowboy books, the only literature in the house, and loved cars so much so that his second job was selling them. Though he had two jobs and Mam worked full-time, we were always skint (had no money). Dad used to spend both time and money on other people he thought were worse off than we were and a family outing always included a few waifs and strays.

The biggest source of anxiety for me when I was growing up was the black bag. The black bag lived on the top shelf of a cupboard in the kitchen. Whatever money we had in the world was in the black bag. The bills, food, Dad's tabs (cigarettes) all came out of the black bag. As I was in the house more than the rest of the family, it was me who had to answer the door to the coalman, the milkman or the window cleaner. It was me who had to check the contents of the black bag and if there was no money, go and say we couldn't pay this week. The biggest anxiety came from being sent to the local shop to get Dad's daily ration of Golden Virginia and green papers. Dad was a compulsive smoker and squeezed his eighty-a-day habit out of his half an ounce of rolling tobacco. If there was no money in the bag, I still had to go to the shop and put it on our tick (debt) tab. If Dad was overdue paying the tick tab, then I had to plead with Mr. Foster, the shopkeeper, to extend the tick. No baccy (tobacco) and Dad's nerves would be on end and tempers would flare.

My mam had a dual personality so I grew up with two mothers. Mam was kind, generous and caring. I loved her deeply. She worked hard to create the best home life for her husband and children. Not only did she work long hours, but our house was always immaculate as she was fiercely house proud and couldn't cope if anywhere was untidy or something was out of place. It was difficult to relax as she policed her home. She saved up for Christmas and birthday presents, keeping the money hidden from Dad. We all had loads of presents, which I thought was a miracle compared to the rest of the year. She had a knack for homemaking with little money and, amongst my friends, we were regarded as posh. Every Friday, after a twelve-hour shift, she would bake bread buns and we would have a

14

midnight feast. That was about all she cooked. Dad did most meals out of his lard-encrusted frying pan and chip pan, a diet that would catch up with us all in later life. Mam had the ability to emotionally switch off when times were hard or a crisis emerged. She would just disconnect and take her mind somewhere else, leaving her body behind. Most people who knew her, regarded her as a sweet, kind lady.

Mam had another personality which I refer to as "Mother". You wouldn't want to mess with Mother who had a wicked temper, could take you out with a single punch and verbally destroy you with her caustic tongue. Mother never appeared very often, but when she did, it was chaotic. Dad and Mother would often row and those rows could easily turn into throwing things or fisticuffs. She would swear and curse, and roll her tongue the same as Granda did when he was angry. It was Dad who always had to step down when Mother was around as she would never give in. One day I came into the house with a fat lip, courtesy of my best friend's big brother punching me in the face. Mother grabbed me by the arm and dragged me across the street to my friend's house. As we got near the house, my friend's dad was in the garden. By the time he looked up, Mother had run at the house, jumped on the wall and laid him out with a single punch. She was a four foot, ten-inch powerhouse. The police were called but when they arrived, Mother had gone and Mam was back - the kind, sweet lady who everyone knew and loved.

On another occasion, I was hiding in the grass in our overgrown back garden, trying to avoid going to the big school where I was being bullied. Our next-door neighbour, Mrs Vaughn, was Mother's spy and when Mother stepped out of the house to go to work, she was tipped off by Mrs Vaughn that I was in the garden. Mother waited until I returned to the house and let myself in with the latch key. She went ballistic, grabbed me by the pocket of my new school blazer and beat the crap out of me. She ripped the pocket clean off and beat me so badly I was black and blue for days and had to stay off school in case she was found out. Mother would disappear as quickly as she would arrive. When Mother beat me, it was Mam who would bathe the wounds and speak softly to me. It was incredibly confusing.

Although we were a dysfunctional family, living with Mam and Dad was ok most of the time. I started visiting our local horse stables when I was four years old and with the five shillings saved up by Mam had my first horse ride. Stan Malam, the owner of the stable, was a womaniser, a crook and was cruel to his horses, his wife and son. That did not deter me. Horses were in my blood and for the next fourteen years, I would go every night to muck the stables out to get free horse rides. With the horses, I could forget about Mother and the black bag.

One Sunday, when I was ten years old, Dad came home and announced he had been "saved" and was now "a born-again Christian." He had been going to the Baptist church in Jarrow and joined the choir because he loved to sing. This Sunday, when the pastor made his monthly altar call, Dad went to the front, accepted Jesus as his personal Saviour, was born again and saved from the wrath of God and the eternal fires of hell. It was a catastrophic event that would turn our ordinary, dysfunctional family into a bunch of religious fruit cakes. Born-again Christianity should have a government health warning because it seriously messes with your head.

Let me explain the religion of the Megalomaniac. The gist of it goes something like this: God made the world and Adam and Eve. They lived in a garden paradise and the only requirement God placed on them was not to eat the fruit of the tree of the knowledge of good and evil. They ate the fruit, got kicked out of paradise and doomed the whole human race to God's wrath and punishment, which was to be tormented and burn in hell for eternity. Because God loves us, he created a people, the Jews, and from that people came a Saviour, Jesus Christ. He was God's only Son, and He sent him from heaven to earth where he would live a life obeying God, unlike Adam and Eve. He would live, then die on a cross, the victim of the Roman and religious authorities. His sacrificial death would appease the wrath of God, pay a ransom to the devil that freed humanity from his clutches. Jesus then destroyed death by being raised from the dead, the third day after his death. This is all summed up in a verse from the gospel of John (3:16, NIV): "For God so loved the world that he gave his one and only Son, that whoever believes in him shall not perish but have eternal life."

If you are not religious, and have got this far, then well done. This way of believing in God results in violence. If you are "saved," the rest of the world is "lost" (and deserving of hell). If you are now part of a holy people and nation, the rest of the world is an evil empire. You now must live a life in keeping with your new status by living a new life in the Spirit, which is following a moral code. In truth, a mixture of the Ten Commandments, ancient Jewish morality laws and the teaching of Jesus and his Apostles. These toxic beliefs would provide the fuel to drive the vehicle that would dump me in the Sunderland Borough Lunatic Asylum. It would also play a significant part in each of the four traumatic incidents that I am writing about in this book.

My dad's concept of g-d was of a loving, forgiving friend and he pretty much rejected the baggage that came with being born again. Born-again Christianity infected most of my family. I got "saved" at a televised Billy Graham rally and went to the front at the altar call to receive Jesus as my personal Saviour. My sister Freda's husband, Trevor, took it on himself to police the family to ensure each one of us was living a "Godly" and "Holy" life and being a good witness for Jesus. It is just a subtle form of repression where the base aspects of human nature are buried under a religious veneer, waiting to re-emerge in unguarded moments. We all attended the Baptist church in Jarrow and later its mission church near our house. Each week, they reinforced the message that we had been saved from the eternal fires of hell by Jesus and that it was our mission to live a good life and be a witness for Jesus. The list of rules and regulations that point to how you should live that good life were endless. They covered simple things like not shopping on Sundays to other issues like divorce, homosexuality and masturbation. There was no mention of social justice, which my granda advocated his whole life. It created a community of self-righteous hypocrites who certainly didn't practice what they preached.

When puberty kicked in and I became more interested in girls than Jesus, I also began to spot the chasm that existed between belief and everyday living. I saw it in the church deacon who would preach against smoking, then nip out for a quick fag (cigarette) followed by a mint and stinky minty breath. Then there were the sexual affairs, the backbiting, the power plays and irruptions of unbridled nastiness. I realised then that I wanted nothing to do with this Megalomaniac God who kept his people in check with threats of violence. I already had Mother to do that.

I knew leaving the church would incur the wrath of my family. The decision, however, was to be made for me. My dad had his first heart attack aged 42. It was massive and nearly killed him. When I visited him in hospital, I could see the despair and deep depression that was taking hold of him. In those days, there was little treatment for the disease behind the attack. Dad knew he had been given a death sentence and he was a dead man walking. The doctor demanded he give up smoking, but not the frying pan, which was probably the main cause of his condition. Mam knew that would be impossible so she bought him a pipe. It only made matters worse as he inhaled the pipe tobacco. Dad was a ticking time bomb: you would never know when he was going to explode, which he did frequently. Eventually, he went back to work, things calmed down for a bit and we slipped back into being a reasonably ordinary dysfunctional family, acted out in the shadow of death. I was at school when they came to tell me. Dad was dead. He was 44. I was 14 years old.

When I arrived home, by brother Alan who is six years older than me, was banging his head off the wall until it bled. Like Mam, he never could cope with the dark side of life. This was his way of grieving. My sister Freda, eight years older than me, and like a second mam, was sitting in the dining room sobbing. She loved her dad deeply. Mam was in the sitting room surrounded by people, some from the church, some friends. She looked up at me and I could see total bewilderment in her eyes. Like Alan, she didn't want to know or handle a tragedy. She was pleading with me to take it away, to make it stop; a look I would get familiar with in the years ahead. I wanted to tell everyone to get the fuck out of our house. Instead, I went upstairs and sat on my bed. There was going to be no tears, only the loosening of a primal anger.

I went with Auntie Freda's husband Eddie to the funeral, refusing to travel in the funeral cars. Eddie was disabled too and had a blue mini converted for him to use. Eddie loved my dad, they were good friends. We drove to the church in silence. There was only room for standing in the church, both floors were full. That's around 500 people. This was way bigger than the church congregation. The fact so many of Dad's friends, workmates and people he had helped turned up was a sign that the g-d he discovered in this church had remained for him a loving and forgiving friend and not the Megalomaniac that was now worshipped here.

The days that followed were full of people visiting Mam to offer their condolences. Few noticed that Mam had taken off to one of her safe places, leaving her body to greet the visitors. When they left, Mam returned, still looking bewildered. In her eyes, she was still asking me what to do. The minister Mr Saspry turned up dressed immaculately in a black jacket, waistcoat and pin stripped trousers, more appropriate for a wedding than a bereavement visit. He adopted his pulpit diction and talked at my mam, telling her God could be trusted and it was His will to take Dad. Mam had already gone to a safe place, leaving me to listen to this fucking nonsense. I wanted to throw this self-righteous, jumped-up, do-gooder out of the house. Dad was 44 for g-d's sake! I had told Mr Saspry not to touch my dad's Yorkshire terrier Sam. As he continued with his blab, blab to the absent Ada (Mam), he reached out to stroke Sam who immediately jumped up and bit him on his rather big nose. It bled profusely down his suit until he found his hanky. He fled the house and Sam and I waited until Mam came back. That event marked the end of my relationship with the Megalomaniac.

With Dad gone, Trevor took leadership of the family and became the voice of God. He couldn't cope with the fact that I had quit as it could eventually be the start of a mutiny. Although I had quit, the Megalomaniac was still messing with my head. I had been thoroughly brainwashed and it would take years to silence that voice. Trevor reinforced it: leaving the flock, I was now doomed for the eternal fires of hell. I decided that if hell was my destination, then I was going to have a good time on the way. My brother Alan gave me ten shillings to go and have my first pint. I went with some friends to the Viking in Jarrow town centre as they turned a blind eye to your age. With ten bob (shillings) I could buy three pints of beer and a packet of ten Embassy Regal. I loved alcohol; it made me feel calm and safe. I was never angry when I drank.

Just before Dad died, I had been bullied by a pupil and teacher at the grammar school. Most of my friends had gone to the secondary school so I asked for a transfer. In the first week at the new school, I was playing football in the yard when one of the bigger lads pushed me over. I jumped up and smashed him in the face. He backed off. I had once again connected with a primal anger that would nearly undo me in the months ahead. I was not going to be bullied again, never again. When I was at infant school, there were two gangs. I led one and Frankie Potts led the other. Every week, he would demand a fight. I would always turn up, get a beating and go back to my gang. Frankie, an even bigger lad now, was at the new school. We became great friends. He made it known that any teacher or pupil who messed with me would have him to deal with. Although I didn't need a body guard, it was a great gesture. I am sure I was made head boy of the school because of my relationship with Frankie.

It was at the new school that I spotted Sandra. She had black hair, deep blue eyes and a great figure for a fourteen-year-old. The only thing was she had a boyfriend who was sixteen. That didn't deter me. I joined the domestic science class so I could get close to her. Eventually she dumped the boyfriend and we got together. Her family hated me. They were middle class and thought I wasn't good enough for her. She lived near our house and on an evening, I would stand at the corner of her street and whistle. She would then appear and we would walk over the motorway bridge to my house. Mam usually had her friend Gladys around on an evening so Sandra and I would either go out or sit in the dining room. On Wednesdays, Mam's friend Peggy would come and take her over to her house for a couple of hours. Sandra and I started to have sex on those Wednesday nights. It was adolescent sex, neither intimate or adventurous. It was usually over in under five minutes. I always used a condom until the night my condom fell out of my hiding place in a cupboard into the floor space underneath. It was impossible to retrieve, but we still had sex.

Mam had become more dependent on me since Dad died and she often called me "Binks," Dad's nickname. Freda and Trevor had gone to Bible College to learn how to serve the Megalomaniac. Alan was married so it was just me and Mam. She had physically deteriorated following Dad's death and was mentally unstable. I had to help her dress, cook, clean, light the fire and do other chores. On good days, when she could move around, she was the first to help as she was still house proud and I couldn't meet her standards. She wanted me to sleep in the same bed with her. I gave in after her pleading. It all started to get a bit strange and so I returned to my own bed. Mother seemed to have disappeared, though I did get the occasional glimpse of her. I was older, bigger and had a temper to reckon with so perhaps that held her back.

Sandra had begun to have doubts about our relationship. My temper was getting the better of me and she witnessed it on two occasions. The first time was when we were in a pub with some friends. The estate bully was in the pub and I was one of his victims. He kicked off with his sarcasm, trying to humiliate me in front of my friends. Then it was the usual: "Let's go outside and fight or are you a coward?" This time I said "ok" and I could see the fear in his eyes. I beat the shit out of him. My friends had to pull me off because I was possessed by my primal anger and could have killed him. He had to go to hospital. A second occasion was at a dance. I had heard one of the bigger boys was going to take me on. I took a knife. I went into the toilet to pee and he appeared with a group of friends, a bully boy tactic. I could feel the anger rising, fuelled by the memories of former bullies. He began to laugh and I pulled out the knife and held it to his throat. He could see I was possessed and ready to kill him. He peed his pants and I think it was then that the demon left me. Then there was the jealousy. I wanted to know everything Sandra was doing, who she had spoken to and if anyone had shown an interest in her. Anyone who had would get a beating. I got the nickname "Psycho Skinner". Sandra had had enough. She was right, she deserved better and she dumped me. I stalked her and threatened any boy who went near her.

One weekend, I was returning from the beach with a wagon full of ponies. I was 16, driving without a license, but Stan Mallam was a crook, all he cared about was making money. I was driving towards a roundabout at Tyne Dock, the halfway point between South Shields and Jarrow when I spotted Sandra walking on the opposite side of the road. She was heavily pregnant. I was so shocked I drove directly over the roundabout. Nobody got hurt and the wagon and ponies were ok. I got back to the farm and swore I would kill the bastard who had got her in the family way. After doing the math, it turned out to be my child. I went to see her and we talked about getting back together. Her father then asked to see me. He said the best thing I could do was walk out of his house and under a bus. He swore I would never see Sandra or my child when he was born.

Sandra gave birth to Andrew. Her dad kept his promise. I kept mine: to kill the bastard who got her in the family way. The first attempt was feeble: a few of Mam's sleeping pills and a stomach pump. The next time was more serious with a lot more pills and a longer stay in hospital. One afternoon, I walked over the motorway bridge I used to cross to see Sandra. I stood in the middle, climbed on the fence and jumped off. I escaped with a twisted ankle and a one-way ticket to Sunderland Borough Lunatic Asylum. I had lost my dad, Sandra and Andrew. I hated the person I had become and couldn't escape the Megalomaniac who was still messing with my head.

When I left Cherry Knowle Hospital (Sunderland Borough Lunatic Asylum), my life spiralled out of control. My nana died of heart failure. She was staying with us, sleeping on the settee so we could watch her and get anything she needed. Watching Nana die was unbelievably emotional. Mam called the doctor out when she saw Nana was struggling. The duty doctor was rude and curt. She looked at Nana who was still conscious and announced she would be dead in hours. I grabbed the doctor by the arm and marched her out of our house. Nana died a few minutes later. I helped carry her upstairs into the back bedroom and sat with her most of the night, combing her hair. Granda died a year or two later. When I got to him, he was spewing blood from a burst artery in his stomach. He was terrified of dying. His son Alec rushed him to hospital. There was nothing they could do. When the family broke up the house, Nana and Granda's house, I felt my childhood was being torn from me.

The only friend I had was alcohol and I would do anything to keep that friendship going. I drifted from job to job, never staying too long or making friends. Casual sex became a big feature of my life and I was never fussy who it was with. Trevor was still on patrol and I goaded him and my sister incessantly. I would deliberately put on television programmes that offended the Megalomaniac and refuse to turn them off.

Mam had remarried and when Big John came along I was free as he took over as man of the house and Mam's carer. He was a serious binge drinker. I lived and worked with him for a time in a garage owned by a family friend. On Fridays, Big John used to put in his wine order for delivery that night. It included six cans of special brew strong lager, a bottle of whisky and ten cigarettes. He would then proceed to drink most of it himself. If I was lucky, I would get a can or two. When he was completely blotto, he would get out a torch and his air gun. We would wait quietly until the mice came out and he would shoot at them. The kitchen was spattered with .22 air rifle pellets.

John was well spoken, dressed in country tweeds and belonged to a well to do family of heavy drinkers and gamblers. I was sent to rescue one of his uncles because the bank had seized his house and were waiting to evict him. The house was filthy. He lived in one room with a mattress on the floor and a fat-ridden portable grill that looked like it had not been used for some time. He was emaciated and stinking. There were whisky bottles everywhere. I was nearly sick as I helped him into my van and the eight-hour journey back up North was an endurance test. John tried to help him, but he got kicked out of lodgings and ended up in a care home. The drink finally got him and, though sad, John was relieved.

As my relationship with DD (Dreaded Drink) deepened, I started coming in later at night or in the early hours of the morning. John would get up and let me in. He never complained, just told me to get off to bed. He wouldn't let Mam get involved at all now. He was absolutely devoted to and doted on Mam. He rarely drank now or smoked.

One afternoon, following a drinking session, I decided with another friend to try some LSD for a laugh. We took the first tab and nothing happened, then a second and a third. What we didn't know was that LSD sometimes take several minutes to kick in. When the hit came, I was completely off my head. LSD or "acid", as it is popularly known, amplifies sounds, colours and visuals. The first couple of hours we spent sitting on a wall watching a glorious light show, it was fantastic. Things then started to get a little darker and I started hallucinating and hearing the voice of the Megalomaniac who was going to kill me. I was freaked out and decided to head for home. Then the channel changed again and a satirical cartoon show opened with Trevor and some of the church folk in it. It was the LSD version of the British TV show 'Spitting Image,' a send-up of the absurdity of the toxic beliefs of the servants of the Megalomaniac.

Arriving home, I met Trevor. The real Trevor kept changing into his cartoon double and I couldn't stop laughing. I ran upstairs to my bedroom and lay down on the bed, closed my eyes and hoped the shows were over. As I started to drift off, I could hear a hissing sound at the bottom of the bed. I looked up to see a long snake ready to attack me. I started to choke. Mam heard me and came to the bedroom. I had my belt around my neck and was pulling it tighter. I thought it was the snake and I was trying to kill it. She took the belt off me. I was still paranoid, and she rang a priest she had met recently and he agreed to come and see me.

David Martineau was a middle-aged man, tall, balding and extremely well spoken. He was Church of England which means he was not born-again. "He is not to be trusted," said the Megalomaniac. Those words played over again as we walked on the beach in South Shields. He didn't talk, he knew that words at this point were futile.

By the early hours of the morning, I was back to reality. We drove to his church and sat near the altar. I could hear the voice of the Megalomaniac saying, "he is not to be trusted." They were fainter now. David asked if I wanted to tell him my story and so it began. He could see I was getting anxious and edgy and suggested I have a cigarette. I got up to go outside. He caught my arm so I sat back down. He went into the church kitchen and brought a saucer that I could use as an ashtray. Nervously, I lit a cigarette and breathed in the smoke. I felt calm and relaxed and continued with my story. When we had finished, the saucer was full of stubs. This was the beginning of a relationship that would profoundly influence my life and begin the escape from the Megalomaniac.

David was not a member of the "born-again fraternity" and their psychotic certainty. In the months and years that followed, I discovered he had a deep and meaningful understanding of g-d that was rooted in a positive uncertainty. He introduced me to Dietrich Bonhoeffer lending me *The Cost of Discipleship*. He described it as the "small print" on the contract of baptism. He explained to me the drama in the Eucharist and the beauty and gravity in the liturgy. He introduced me to the mystical tradition and monasticism. He stressed the importance of social justice and inclusion of people different to ourselves.

Two years before I met David, he had been in the throes of a deep depression. One day, a man knocked on the vicarage door and asked to see the vicar. David showed him into the study and asked why he had come. Norman told a story of being locked in a deep depression and how he wanted to kill himself. As a last resort, he called out to g-d to help him. He describes being overwhelmed by an unconditional love and when the experience ended, the darkness that had engulfed him was gone. He explained to David that he was unsure what had happened to him and thought he should tell David about it. David spoke about his own depression and how it was paralysing his ministry. Norman asked if it might be a good idea if they prayed together and ask g-d to help. As they prayed that same unconditional love filled the study, once again overwhelming

Norman and this time David too. It lasted for some time.

When it was over, both Norman and David were asking the same question: "Wow, what happened there?" They came up with the same answer: "unconditional love." Later that day, David asked Norman if he would come and share his story at the church and later in the Eucharist they would pray together with anyone who wanted to take part. As they prayed, unconditional love overwhelmed most of the members of the congregation. They went home and told their families and soon the church was packed on Sundays and at the Wednesday bible study. David refused to name or try to explain what was going on, letting people decide for themselves if this was connected to g-d. I started going to church on Sundays, motivated by the fact there were some seriously attractive ladies in the congregation. I witnessed these phenomena several times, but remained sceptical.

One night, I went to what I thought was going to be a young people's evening and, to my dismay, it was a prayer group. There was only David and a middle-aged couple Dorothy and Jimmy, who were always supportive of me. I felt trapped by kindness and I knew I had to stay.

My experience of prayer meetings wasn't good. I was used to people shouting and stirring things up as they pleaded with the Megalomaniac to save the world. This was slightly different, nobody said a word. It was unnerving and when I saw David, then Dorothy and Jimmy slip into their unconditional love mode, I decided it was time to slip out the door. I tried to stand up, but I couldn't move. Had I had a stroke or some other paralysing event? I was nervous, frightened and panicked. I tried to shout out to David, but the words would not come out. Then a warm presence settled on me. Instead of fighting the paralysis, I settled into it and began to relax and to rest. I felt so much stress and anxiety lift off me. The more I relaxed and trusted what was going on, the deeper the whole experience became. I began to see into my past, to times with Mother, but they could not disturb this unconditional love. I wanted this to last forever; the DD and LSD together came nowhere close to what was happening here. This was a peace and a love I had never experienced before. Then I heard a whisper from deep inside of me: "It's not your fault, it's not your fault, it's not your fault." The floodgates opened and I began to weep and weep. I couldn't stop. I didn't want to stop. These tears were cleansing, healing, transforming.

When the tap was turned off, I was aware that David, Dorothy and Jimmy had been waiting patiently for my return. It was 11.30pm. I had been sitting there for four hours. David offered to take me home. I went to stand up, but couldn't make it. My body was no longer paralysed, but more like a floppy doll. My limbs had relaxed so much that my arms and legs were just not coordinated. David and Jimmy offered to help me out to the car. Each placed a hand under my arm and carried me out to the car, my legs dragging behind. It was ten minutes to my house. When we arrived, I still couldn't walk. Mam answered the door. David explained what had happened and offered to carry me to the house and upstairs to bed. By this time, I had started laughing uncontrollably as the tension oozed out of my body. Mam was convinced I was drunk and no reassurance from David made any difference.

I slept like a baby, but woke up to one serious hangover. Megalomaniac was back with a vengeance, parading before me every memory that was needed to prove I was a shit person. Yes, it was my fault. I rang David to ask him what to do. He explained this was something that often followed an experience that we shared the night before. He felt I was strong and able to withstand this assault. However, he suggested we begin to look for a person or an organisation that could provide me with some therapy to deal with the demons.

Parkwood House was an alcohol and drug addiction centre in Gosforth, around ten miles from Jarrow. It was led by Dr Alan Freed, an innovative psychiatrist, who wasn't afraid to challenge fixed notions relating to the nature and treatment of addiction. There was a waiting list. My GP agreed to put me on it. Eventually I was admitted for a three-month treatment program. There were different types of therapy and I was assigned to group therapy. Dr Freed had pioneered a methadone programme as part of a plan to enable heroin users to break their addiction. I met my friend Benny when he was on that programme and admitted for additional therapy. To be honest, I think our friendship prevented us from really doing the work that was needed to get the benefit from the therapy. There was also one major distraction: a very attractive sex addict in my group. She was predatory and during her stay conquered most of the male patients. It was a contributing factor to the failure of my first term of therapy. At the end, the group leader asked me into her office. She made it very clear that the work had not even begun and recommended I seek another term as soon as possible. I thought I had done well. Going back to Jarrow revealed my total failure. Fortunately, I managed to get on another term.

I mentioned in the introduction that I planned to write this book as a series of psychoanalytical events, not as a common-sense chronological story. I want to explain that a little further. When I returned to Parkwood

House, Benny had started primal scream therapy which involved revisiting traumatic memories, connecting to the emotions and screaming out the pain attached to them. During one session, he recalled an incident that took place in a public toilet, in Brighton, at Christmas. He was looking for a vein that hadn't collapsed so he could inject heroin. He found one on the knuckle on his hand. While injecting, the needle broke. His hand swelled and infection set in. When recalling that memory, the same thing happened: his hand swelled and had the appearance of an infection. It stayed like that for several minutes. During my first session at Parkwood House, I was telling the common-sense story of my life. The challenge this time around was to embrace the psychoanalytical event. It would mean recalling the event and experiencing the emotions attached to it and the pain. This session of therapy demanded it.

The next three months were the most intensive emotional experiences I had ever encountered. Recognising my willingness to cooperate this time around, the team began to deconstruct my common-sense story. No stone was left unturned, no path not followed. They concentrated on my experience with the Megalomaniac, his followers and Mother. They even asked Mother to come to the centre to talk to one of the therapists. Mam came several times, but Mother never showed up. The therapists were aware of this, but couldn't push any harder. By the time my therapy had finished, I was aware of an unconscious mantra that was running under the surface of my consciousness: "It's all your fault." We concluded that this was the voice of an undisclosed emotional trauma that was linked to Mother. More work would be required later.

During my stay, the therapists used to take some of us out to drink alcohol socially. Dr Freed argued that if you wrongly diagnose a person as an alcoholic, then the patient will be obliged to inhabit the condition. Freed distinguished between alcoholism and alcohol abuse, the latter as the result of self-medication to treat the pain of trauma. Most mental health specialists would deny that position, arguing alcoholism is a progressive illness. Unlike AA, where having a single drink after a period of abstinence is seen to be falling off the wagon (which works for many people), Dr Freed's way advocated, during times of stress, to drink socially every three days to keep the alcohol level up. When the stress is over, you can then stop. This would not be good for everyone, but in my case, it has saved my life and given me the stability to marry, have four kids, five grandchildren, embrace a vocation and face head on further traumas that were coming my way.

2. GLITTERING IMAGES

I decided not to return home when I left Parkwood House. Big John was now Mam's full-time carer so I was free to follow my own way.

Benny and I rented a flat in nearby Jesmond. The flat was the former sitting room of a four floor Victorian terraced house. It was split into two rooms with a kitchen and toilet on the next floor up. Benny and I had a bedroom each. On the top floor were a group of working girls and we would often get woken up at night by their clients. Jesmond was a predominantly student area with most houses divided up into rentals. A couple of the working girls were paying their way through college by renting themselves out at night and weekends. Benny and his brother Richie were gifted guitarists and had a band of groupies. There was never a shortage of girls around the house. With little money, there was no falling back into old ways.

I started to wonder what to do with my life. The answer to that question was literally around the corner when once again I met Rev. David Martineau, the priest who would later become my mentor. I was surprised to see him, but could tell from his body language and sad face that something was wrong. His eight-year-old son Timothy had an aggressive form of bowel cancer, which David would also suffer from and overcome some years later. The Church was very supportive and was confident that unconditional love would win the day; David was less sure. He would call at the house to chat or just sit quietly, preparing himself for what now seemed inevitable.

When Timothy died, his grief was heart-breaking. We both knew that unconditional love seemed to be impotent in the face of such suffering and this seemed to be an integral part of the whole experience. We also knew that unconditional love was in the suffering and was not the cause of it, whereas Mr Saspry saw death as an outworking of God's will. We saw it as an enemy who robbed us of people we loved. There was no answer that would be good enough to any question of why? No questions meant no lies and we could work through the grief and uncertainty following the loss

27

of loved ones.

In one of our conversations about faith and meaning, David asked if I had thought about training as a priest. My immediate response, "Me a priest? You must be joking!" He wasn't and asked me to think about it. In the days ahead, it became the main thing going on in my head. I had lost interest in the girls, the parties. Benny was a great friend, but I sensed this was going to be the parting of ways, for the present at least.

There was a Methodist church opposite the house and I decided to go to a Sunday service. The Megalomaniac was present, though his violent potential was carefully hidden behind a sickly-sweet demeanour of peace and love. I left half way through. Back at the flat, I connected into my primal anger and this time it was directed at the bullying Megalomaniac. The hatred was intense and the swearing and cursing was shocking, even for me. At the end of it, I was exhausted but there was no relief. I sat at the window, smoking cigarettes and gazing absent-mindedly into the street. Then I had a moment.

You will notice in my writing that when I speak personally about God, I use g-d. So many atrocities have been carried out in the name of God, by people who have a psychotic certainty that they are acting in the name of God or are manipulating the name of God to legitimise their own ambitions. When I use the name of g-d, I am inviting you to join with me and try to understand events in our lives that have a synchronicity: when outward and inward events come together in a way that challenges our everyday understanding of how things work and take us to a new level of awareness. We sometimes describe them in the following ways as: "a bit of luck," "it came out of the blue," "I had a moment." The moment I had that day in the flat in Jesmond was the conviction that Megalomaniac, the tyrannical, all-powerful and cruel God, was not the same as the g-d of unconditional love. Megalomaniac is God with a capital G. Unconditional love is impotent in the tragic events in our lives, but is present in them in a way that makes them unable to defeat us and has the potential to transform us. This is a scary love, an unconditional love with no need to threaten or intimidate and equally no need to be explained or to be understood. I wanted to find out more and decided to follow David's lead and see if being a priest was the way to go.

Foolishly, I took it on myself to make the first application. I wrote a friendly letter to the Bishop of Jarrow, Alexander Hamilton, sharing a few details about my life and asking for details about how I might be tested for ordination as a priest. I received a rather cold and concise reply that stated I was not Church of England material and lacked the academic requirements. To climb over this first obstacle, I needed a theological education. Trevor and my sister Freda had studied theology at Lebanon Missionary Bible College in Berwick-on-Tweed, which is a border town between England and Scotland. It was hinted to me that if I applied, I might be accepted. I sent off a letter to the principal Dr Rigby and waited for the reply. You can see from the name of the college that I felt like I was walking into a Megalomaniac trap.

The interview day came. I borrowed a suit from my brother. The trousers were two sizes too big with a beer stain on the crotch. Aunty Doris bought me socks and a pair of plastic dress shoes. I bought a shirt and tie and headed north for the interview. There were no nerves, group therapy had sharpened my listening skills and gave me an uncanny ability to suss out where people were coming from very quickly.

Dr Rigby was of medium build, in his fifties, with a crop of light coloured hair. He had an irritating habit of sniffing and burying his nose in a handkerchief, a common habit of hay fever sufferers and cocaine users. I took to him immediately. He was a sincere bloke who had spent many years in India and Africa as a medical doctor/missionary working amongst the poorest people. He cared about people.

Rev. Douglass Patterson was a small man who wore tweeds and tartans and sported a bald head with an outcrop of ginger hair. A reformed Anglican, a former public-school boy, with an accent to go with it and a Scottish aristocratic air about him. Douglass wouldn't recognise a feeling or an emotion until it bit him on the bottom.

Rev. Peter Collinson was very friendly and smiled a lot. I became aware very quickly that the glittering image that I was seeing at this moment in time was not the real thing. I would have to wait to meet the real man.

David Holliday was the college bursar, a tough job as the whole place was run on a wing and a prayer. David had an unusual accent, a high-pitched drawl where he dragged out his vowels. I liked David and thought his work for the college was undervalued and, like all of them, underpaid.

Interview over, I was asked to wait in the corridor while they decided my fate. On my return, I discovered both Rev. Collinson and Rev. Patterson were opposed to me joining them. They felt I didn't have what it takes to complete the three-year course and my moral outlook could seriously damage the college's reputation and their witness in the community. Dr Rigby and Mr Gardener had a different point of view. Although they shared the concerns of their colleagues, Dr Rigby reminded them that the college, via Freda and Trevor, had prayed that God would bring me back to the fold so they were in no position to turn me away.

I returned to Jesmond and started to do what was needed to make it all happen. I managed to secure a grant to fund part of the course fees, plus some daily living allowance. My mam, Freda and Trevor were delighted: the lost sheep had returned. I felt more like a wolf in sheep's clothing.

College was everything I had anticipated it to be. It was an almost identical culture to what I had experienced in the church of Megalomania. The main building was a grand Georgian mansion. The women were accommodated on the first floor. Downstairs there was a library, sitting room, dining room, kitchen and pantry. The building adjacent to the house was built in the late 60s, a very simple concrete and wooden rectangular box, decidedly ugly. Upstairs were the men's dormitories which were very uniform and utilitarian. Downstairs were the lecture rooms, meeting places and offices.

I have belonged to several religious communities and noted that they have an outward appearance, "the glittering image", that is presented to society and an inward reality, how they are behind closed doors. The idea of being a witness for Jesus is closely linked to outward appearance, that is where the emphasis is placed. It is required that we be on our best behaviour, showing a sound moral character so those outside the Christian community will see Jesus in us. Can you imagine the pressure creating your own "glittering image"? Jacques Lacan, a French philosopher and psychoanalyst, has a good take on this.

In his seminar *The Four Fundamental Concepts of Psychoanalysis* (1978), Jacques Lacan talks about being caught in the gaze of the Other. I discovered what he meant when Linda and I went to Nicaea, in Turkey. We visited the Basilica which was the venue to the first Christian Council in AD 325. Most of the wall icons had been defaced either by the iconoclastic movement in the Church, which believed God and the Saints should not be visibly represented. Alternatively, it could have been the triumph of Islam in the area, which shared the same belief that there should be no images of God. Walking around the Basilica I noticed a hole in the ground which had an iron bar grid not unlike a drain. I knelt to peep inside. It was pitch black. As I became accustomed to the dark, I suddenly felt undone. I was caught in the gaze of another, in this case, an icon of Jesus. As I stared into his eyes and looked at his face, I could sense his deep vulnerability. This was the meaning of community for me to get caught in the gaze of the Other, when we are caught off guard, not when we are behaving ourselves, stripping us of our "glittering images." I was touching the divine impotence, which I had begun to experience was at the very heart of the sacred anarchy of the kingdom of g-d, the violence of love in the face of hatred and collective evil. I longed to understand more about the relationship between divine impotence and sacred anarchy.

College life revolved around a daily routine: roll call was at 6.am. Chores like peeling potatoes and cleaning started at 6.30am. Breakfast was at 7.30am and chapel at 8.15am. The day was then spent in lectures from 9.15am until 4.30pm with breaks for coffee, the loo and lunch. Dinner was at 5.30pm. You were required to eat everything that was put in front of you as part of your missionary training when you may find yourself in a country with a different food culture. Fortunately, Lorna was a great cook. Rev. Patterson used to bring a little bag with a food alternative in case there was something on his plate he didn't want to eat. He would balance the bag on his knee and swap it with the offending food. I loved the wry smile that came over him when the transgression was complete as if he had got away with it, the naughty boy. Study began at 6.30pm. It was a three-hour stint that was obligatory. A light supper was served at 9.30pm. Lights went out at 10.30pm.

On Friday evenings, we had our mission night. We had missionaries from all over the world telling us their stories. There were stories I found deeply challenging and moving such as those from missionaries who had laid aside their own ambitions to share in another's suffering and trials. Most of them, however, I found disturbing, particularly those of parents putting themselves and their children in danger for an ideology/belief that was consuming them. Saturday was our day off. Sunday was church all day, either preaching, teaching at Sunday school or just attending.

We were a right mixed bunch of people: from dour Scots to intense Englishmen, an occasional Welshman and a sprinkling of international students. I settled into the routine of college life and started to make some friends. I shared a room with Nigel, a rather shy lad and an industrious student. He had a wry sense of humour and was fun to be around. You had to bring your own sheets, blankets and bedcovers. My sheets were purple, the bedcover was yellow and my pyjamas were red. He said he needed to wear sunglasses to sleep.

I first spotted Linda when she was working in the college kitchen. I had been chasing another girl who turned out to be at bit of a schoolmarm, not my type. There were a couple of lively girls who were a bit worldly wise. I decided to concentrate on the studying. Linda had other ideas. I started to teach guitar class and she turned up for every lesson. My best friend at college, John Winter, was a middle-aged man. He had lived several lives so was on my wave length. He was also my cigarette buddy and we would nip out for a quick smoke. I eventually stopped because it was so cold outside. He organised a trip to Bamburgh beach and invited a few friends along. Linda hitched a ride. We chatted on the beach and at the café at nearby Belford. She had a rusty old red mini so she and I used to head off on local excursions and a romance began to blossom. Linda was petite, fair haired with sparkling green eyes. Her beautiful smile could light up a room, a sign of the genuine person she was.

A couple of months into the relationship, Linda gave me an ultimatum: either this relationship was going somewhere or it was over. Whoa, hold your horses, that is all a bit fast for me! She gave me a brief time to think it over. One evening, we were walking from the town up the hill back to the college. We then had a moment, not expected or anticipated. We were caught in a bubble where our feelings were amplified and the night sky took on a luminous quality, the stars dancing and vibrating. This was the moment that sealed the deal. There was no question about it, we both had met our other half.

Linda and I come from similar backgrounds, although her family life was more stable. Her dad Wilf was twenty-two years older than Marjorie, Linda's mum. Wilf was a quiet bloke but could become pedantic and dogmatic about the rules of everyday life. Linda often felt squashed by his strong opinions. He had fought in World War I, mostly in North Africa and the Middle East. He seldom talked about his experiences but they had hardened his views about human depravity and the cruelty of God. Like my dad, when he left the army, he had no skills so he took any jobs available from chauffeuring to long distance lorry driving. His first marriage failed. His ex-wife took their two children to New Zealand. It was a major blow for him, though the two girls would seek their dad out in later years.

When Wilf married Marjorie, he found an absolute gem. They had three kids: Averil first, then four years later, the twins, Linda and Peter. They lived in the same house that Wilf had shared with his first wife. It was a red brick terraced house with a front room, dining room and kitchen. Upstairs there were three bedrooms and a bathroom. Outside was a backyard and at the front, a tiny garden with an iron grid that led down to the coal cellar. This was in Sale, near Manchester in the industrial north west of England. Wilf and Marjorie shared the same values as my nana and granda: a positive work ethic, a daily routine, moral values, a commitment to family and to looking out for people who needed help.

When Averil and her husband Roger decided to emigrate to New Zealand, Linda followed them for a temporary stay, which ended up lasting two years. She was eighteen years old. Roger was pragmatic with strong opinions he liked to voice. Roger, like Wilf, was very pushy with his views. Linda saw New Zealand as a respite, a place to find herself. After a couple of months, she left Roger and Avril and headed out on her own adventure. She took occasional work to support herself and flat shared to put a roof over her head. Her picture of the world grew as she travelled New Zealand's beautiful and volcanic landscape.

Growing up, Linda would be constantly harassed by her twin Peter to become part of the religious sect both he and her mum belonged to. Peter, like Trevor, had taken on the role of the voice of God and was determined "to save" Linda, Averil and Wilf from this evil world. Like me, Linda recognised the violence in the Megalomaniac and rejected any invitation to get involved. It did, however, stir something in her to ask more questions about the meaning of life.

Towards the end of her travels, Linda had a moment which she had not expected nor was she prepared for. She was walking in the street when unconditional love turned up, not the best place to have an epiphany. She headed back to the flat she shared with Megan. Overcome with an overwhelming feeling of love and acceptance, the logical thing to do was to go and tell people. She also decided she needed to give up her flat and belongings and follow a new path. Megan was worried by this and called the police. Linda was taken to the local mental health hospital where she had previously worked, suspected of having a psychotic breakdown.

After four weeks, she was allowed home, a little deflated, but still keen to understand what had happened to her. She spotted some religious sisters in the street and decided to meet up with them. In the following weeks, they helped Linda to make sense of her recent experience. The sisters encouraged Linda to return home and test her vocation of joining the religious life. She went back to Roger and Averil's, worked in a bank to raise her fare home and was mentored by Marty, a monk, who helped her unwrap the events of the last few months. Back in the UK, she decided to get some theological education. Marjorie was very supportive and together they got it down to two choices for college. I am so glad Marjorie pushed Linda in the direction of Berwick-upon-Tweed.

After our moment on the hill, we wanted to get married as soon as possible. Easter was the next college break so we opted for then. Linda's mum asked for more time to arrange the wedding as Wilf's health had deteriorated. We settled on the 9th July 1977. I hate weddings, so much tension and turmoil. Kevin, my best friend and best man, arrived late after the exhaust fell off his car. He was stressed out and I had to give him a couple of brandies to calm him down (You will remember it was Kevin's dad who Mother had laid out with a single punch). He was the manager of a Burton's Menswear shop in Jarrow. That explains why he arrived in a very nice, discounted suit with eighteen-inch flared bottom trousers.

Trevor, my brother-in-law, was going to marry us, but was having a nervous breakdown so he couldn't make it. His stand-in was the local Methodist circuit minister, John Penny. He was identical to an old boss of mine who had taken the credit and the commission for a contract I had won, supplying thirty-eight temporary building workers to a local building contractor. Throughout the service, I had to avoid eye contact with him in case he aroused the anger intended for another person. It was a low-key wedding, in the Methodist church, with a reception in the hall. My mam and Big John, David and Sara Martineau, and our college friends John and Marg Patterson, joined us. The remainder were Linda's friends, family and neighbours. The hall was set out in the traditional way with the head table for the bridal party and adjoining tables for guests. Marjorie's two neighbours, Mima and Lilian, decided to join the wedding table taking up their place mats and laying them directly in front of Linda and I. This unexpected and disruptive event was a sign of the kind of hospitality that would define our lives in the future.

Tedious Ted, Marjorie's brother, had stepped in to represent Wilf, Linda's dad who was ill and could not attend. Rumour is Tedious Ted was still giving his speech when people began to leave and the tables were being packed up. Linda and I had left earlier in an old Triumph 2000. Linda's mum had bought it so she could learn how to drive.

We headed for the Lake District and the village of Ambleside. We arrived early enough to hire a rowing boat and spent the very sunny afternoon on Lake Windermere, then back to the B&B for an early night. We both had sunburn so the night would be spent on our backs, unable to move. At breakfast, we were greeted by the usual smiles and winks reserved for honeymooners. Linda is a literary groupie and one of her all-time greats is John Ruskin so that day was spent at his historic home in Coniston. Recovered from our sunburn, we were looking forward to a night of passion. The bed was wicked. The mattress was soft and springy and the wooden bed frame was rickety and made the most ridiculous noises with the slightest movement. We missed this the night before, immobilised by sunburn. The following day, we decided to head back and settle into our new home in Berwick-upon-Tweed.

Lily Bowl was a legend in the Berwick community. She and her sister inherited several properties in the town and a financial legacy. The spinster sisters used their money to promote their Christian faith and support charitable enterprise. Lily and her sister lived in a three-story town house just off the main street. Downstairs was the 'Big Knickers' shop where the sisters offered a discreet service making underwear and corsets for the larger lady. It also doubled up as a mission hall when Lily would play her portable organ and her sister would preach to the lost. The sign across the 'Big Knickers' shop read: *Jesus, The Way, The Truth, The Life*. They lived on the middle floor and when her sister died, Lily began to let out the third floor for a bit of company. When Linda and I moved in, Lily was in her eighties. She still did the occasional big knicker thing, mostly corsets.

The shop was no longer a mission hall, but Legend Lily still held onto her religious beliefs and was eager to share them with everyone and anyone. The flat had a small living room that looked out onto a brick wall. You couldn't swing a cat in the kitchen but it was big enough to cook for two. We had two good sized bedrooms so we could put friends up.

Benny, my roommate in Jesmond, and his girlfriend Jane were our first visitors. Benny and Jane stood out like a sore thumb in conservative Berwick. Benny was a medium built lad, with a skinhead haircut and two front teeth missing. He had the obligatory tattoo spots on his cheek, a sign of a crazy life leading to prison. He always wore t-shirts and faded denim jeans, ragged at the bottom, with sandals and no socks (I remember the uniform well!) The t-shirts let him show his muscles and the rest of his tattoo collection. Although he looked menacing, he was a pussy cat. Jane was more Parisian style without the money. She wore tight jeans and vests and let her breasts hang out in complete freedom. She liked to sit on Legend Lily's step, the front door to the flats, smoking cigarettes and soaking up the sun. I was impressed by how warm and friendly Legend Lily was to Ben and Jane. Watching Jane on the step, with *Jesus The Way, The Truth, The Life* above her head, seemed strangely appropriate.

We kicked off college in September. This was my second year and Linda's last year. Dr Rigby was a gifted lecturer and biblical theology was his thing. Because we were taking external examinations, the teaching had to show no bias to a single point of view so we got the benefit of being exposed to current theological trends, which I found extremely exciting. Like most recently married folk, Linda and I were still unpacking both the physical and emotional suitcases that we brought to the marriage. My cases were full of dirty washing, most of which was still connected to Mother. My therapists warned me that as I got closer to the dark secret, my emotions would get more intense. Linda guessed early on that I had a Mother complex. Mam loved Linda; Mother was hostile. The day Mam, Mother and Linda met was awkward. Linda carried dog poo into the house on her shoe and walked it over the freshly hoovered trophy carpet. Mam was so reassuring, "Don't worry pet, it's not a problem." Linda was aware of another presence, one less accepting and positively charged and angry. The fact Linda recognised the duality of Mam and Mother was a great help to me and our relationship together.

In a community where a core value is no sex before marriage, when you do get married, your status goes up a notch. You have crossed over into the forbidden zone and now you know the dark secret of carnal knowledge. College life was ordered and arranged to keep you a virgin. Not long before we joined the college community, the sexes were separated, in chapel, at meal times and in lectures. Of course, laws and prohibitions not only ignite desire, they enflame it. Passions were always simmering under the surface, calmed by having the recommended cold shower or praying more to Jesus. I remember a book was passed around that had a chapter on marriage and sex, by a Christian writer, of course. Within two weeks, it was dog-eared and had some dubious staining. Masturbation was a deadly sin. I learned long ago that laws and prohibitions are the tools of Megalomania. First ignite the fire, then dare you to enjoy it. Unconditional love demands you grow up and make decisions for yourself based on the good of the other.

John and Marg Patterson were our best pals at college. They had steered me through my various meltdowns. I was once very distraught by the repression in the college and the damage it was doing to people. Rita was in her thirties and I watched her slowly descend the psychic ladder towards a break. She was getting up in the early hours to pray and walking around reciting scripture. I warned Dr Rigby but it was too late the break came and she had to be sectioned to a mental health facility. I stood up in the chapel and let rip. Dr Rigby apologised for my outburst and said that I was under a lot of stress and had mental health issues. John and Marg took me home, calmed me down and let me unpack the anger. Linda had built her own relationship with them.

John and Marg were really pleased when we got engaged, unlike Linda's other close friends who knew me from Jarrow. They warned her I was a bad boy and she needed to keep away from me. John and Marg were always there for us when we got married. John had sung at our wedding and they were g-d parents to Jayne, our first child. John and Marg were cool, not at all part of the fuddy-duddy college culture. They were good looking, dressed well and willing to take risks if life presented them. John was my hero, the person who I looked up to most.

Roy and Shirley Searle started college the same time as me. Roy very quickly established himself as head boy, an unofficial role that was bestowed upon the most promising student of good moral character. The last head boy had a glittering image that was one of a calm and prayerful person. Turned out he was a paedophile. Roy and I were about the same age. If he was the blue-eyed boy, I was the bad boy. When he was accepted for ordination into the Baptist church, there were celebrations in the college led by Dr Rigby. When I was accepted for ordination into the Church of England, the Dr congratulated me privately with the comment, "the C of E takes anybody these days."

Like most young men, Roy was competitive, a trait I shared and would regard as healthy. Under the good guy exterior, I spotted an unbridled ambition. I wondered how far he would go to achieve his goal. I found the answer to that the hard way, later down the line. Together, Roy and Shirley were social climbers. Shirley was climbing out of her working-class roots; Roy was reaching much further up the social ladder for a very different set of reasons. Social climbers are always looking for relationships where the other person has something to offer that can help them on their way. Being the rough diamond, neither Roy nor Shirley saw myself or Linda as friends; we had nothing to offer. Years later, when I was developing my work on new monasticism, Roy turned up at my door. This time I had something he wanted.

We met Andy Raine at one of the missionary nights at college. You either love or loathe Andy, there is no middle ground. He wandered into the meeting in a long trench coat and his signature baggy trousers. He was tall and slim with black curly hair and a long face. Andy demands attention and all eyes were on him when he entered the room. People just couldn't work him out. We spoke briefly, it wasn't a memorable meeting. Little did Linda and I know then that our lives would become entwined with Andy's for the next forty years.

Linda and I had lots of friends in Berwick, both in the college and the wider community. The reason I have brought these people to your attention is because our lives would be inextricably caught up in theirs, right up to the present day. More importantly, each would contribute directly to two of the traumatic incidents recorded in this book that Linda, my family and I are still recovering from.

Towards the end of our first year of marriage, we discovered Linda was pregnant. We were out for dinner with some friends when she became dizzy and nauseous. Our friends, experienced in these matters, suggested Linda have a pregnancy test. I was shocked but so chuffed that we were having a baby. It was a tough pregnancy with frequents bouts of sickness. In those unenlightened days, we were thrown off a bus when Linda was sick, mostly over me.

We decided to move to a new house, the second most testing life experience after pregnancy. One day I took a detour while walking home from college. I found an empty house. It was half of what had once been a Georgian Town House, built by a rich merchant. The house looked semi-derelict in comparison to its other half, which was owned and had been renovated by a local builder. I discovered this half of the house, known as Ravensdown, was owned by the local council and made an appointment to see the housing manager. He laughed when I asked if I could rent it, there was no chance! I am persistent so went to see him every week. Finally, I convinced him that it was better to let the house to a poor student than let it deteriorate any further.

The house was huge and our flat would fit into its sitting/dining room. The next room was a former library, again palatial. Both had wooden floors and wood panelling half way up each wall and carved wooden fireplaces. The kitchen was small in comparison with a wash house next to it that was freezing in winter. We washed the terry towelling nappies in there, no Pampers then. The grand staircase led out of the sitting room and onto the first floor. In the middle, the stairs went both to the left and to the right. If you turned left, they led to a brick wall, built when the house was divided. If you turned right, it led to two bedrooms and the family bathroom, a giant space with a loo, bath and wash basin huddled together in one corner. A second, less grand staircase led to a further two bedrooms in the attic. I had absolutely no money, no furniture and no idea what to do. That's when g-d and synchronicity kicked in.

First, we had a random message from friends of Linda in Sale, Manchester. They were off to theological college and wanted to know if we needed their furniture, for free. Great, yes please! But now we had to go and get it. My brother Alan called up to see how we were doing and offered to help. I told him about the furniture in Sale. He arranged and paid for the removal van to collect and deliver it. Local community folk got wind of our new house and offered to help clean and paint where needed. Most brought the paint and brushes and we ended up with some interesting colours in the bedrooms. In the middle of all this activity, Linda had to go to a hospital in Ashington, an hour's drive away. Jayne, our new daughter, was feet first rather than head first so Linda was required to have a caesarean section. She is so afraid of hospitals, so this was a major ordeal. In those days, the midwives were firmly in charge and men were seen but not heard.

At the house, we needed to get finished for mum and baby arriving. I managed to get a social welfare grant and one of the things I bought was a turquoise square of carpet to fill the middle of the sitting room. When the furniture arrived from Sale, most of the sitting room stuff was blue, so it was a great fit. We were still short of lots of items. One of our college friends called around. She was going to take a year out of college and needed somewhere to store the furniture from her rented house. We could use everything; all the gaps were filled. We were ready for Linda and baby.

Jayne was born on the 27th November 1978. She had a punk rocker black hair style and eyes that followed you everywhere. It was proposed that Linda spend some time at the Castle Hills Maternity Home in Berwick, just near our house. I was a little concerned because Linda was not herself. What began next was a five-year nightmare.

Puerperal psychosis or post-partem depression affects one in a thousand women after the birth of a child. In our day, there was no correct diagnosis or treatment. Normal, healthy women start hearing voices, hallucinating and experiencing paranoia. It is incredibly scary and comes and goes in its intensity. Often women would end up in a mental institution, some commit suicide. Having had first-hand experience, there was no way I was going to let that happen to Linda. At its worst, sufferers may be unable to sleep for days on end, haunted by images and voices. Imagine that you are unable to discern if all the random thoughts that go through your head are true or false. It is only exhaustion that allows sleep, only to wake and the cycle begins again. Strange behaviour occurs, usually as a response to the voices such as going outside in night clothes or hiding in cupboards.

Today, puerperal psychosis responds well to the new treatments now available. It is thought that it is the result of an overload of the hormone dopamine. Medication can now get the illness and its devastating symptoms under control in a matter of days, with recovery in six to eight months. I am sharing this information with you because I do not plan to write about the number of times Linda was overtaken by this illness. Rather, it is to give you an idea of the kind of challenges we would be facing over the next five years, with puerperal psychosis providing the background music.

When Linda and I first married, we decided to spend some time at the Society of St. Francis, at their Alnmouth Friary in Northumberland. The Friary was originally built as a bachelor pad for a rich merchant. It is perched on a hill overlooking Alnmouth beach and the sometimes raging North Sea. It is a spectacular space and setting. It is tradition to go and spend some time with a religious community to seek "a word" for your life, a clue as to what g-d would have you collaborate in.

Linda and I agreed not to speak during daylight hours. I spent most of my time sitting in the bay window of the library with amazing views over the sand and sea. The smell of incense from the daily Eucharist lingered throughout the day, in every corner of the Friary. I found the aroma soothing and comforting. Linda liked to walk the beach, something we would do frequently in the future when working out challenges. The band of brothers were very supportive and welcoming and in the years to come we would build a strong bond with them. At the end of our time, we sat down to see if any single word had come to mind. Much to our surprise, we both said the same thing: "community".

The day Linda came home from the maternity hospital, we had a note delivered on behalf of Andy Raine, the lad we had met at a missionary meeting. He was returning from a school in Canada and wondered if he could stay with us for a couple of days. We agreed, with no other motive than to help him out. Andy ended up staying several months.

Ravensdown became a hub for many people, local and from a distance. Our local vicar Canon Donald McNaughton and his curate John Newsome agreed to celebrate Holy Communion at Ravensdown on a Wednesday evening. It was a mixed bunch who attended from all denominations. Dour Dougie, the carrot topped Scot who had made it his personal mission to see me born again, started coming. To his utter surprise, he started to enjoy it. These were the years when the troubles in Northern Ireland were at their height and had spilled onto the streets in the UK, with bombings and assassinations. Catholics killed Protestants in the name of God and Protestants returned the favour. This was the Megalomaniac at its best, stirring up violence and delivering it wrapped up in a religious garment. We made it a condition of coming to Ravensdown that when you stepped in the front door, you left your beliefs outside and picked them up again when you left. No exceptions.

Andy is a people-magnet who would travel the length and breadth of the UK and the USA teaching contemporary dance for use in the context of mission. Andy wasn't a big fan of the Megalomaniac, though like all of us who had been entrapped by the beast, was still trying to work through its negative influences. Andy carried his life possessions, including his bookshop in a set of battered suitcases tied together with string. He hitchhiked everywhere, refusing to contemplate getting a driving license, making long-term contacts and friends with everyone he met. One of the things I liked about him was his ability to treat everyone, whatever their social background, as an equal neither to be courted or treated as a case in question. He used to hang out with a group of folks who lived in one of the most deprived areas of Alnwick. Every Wednesday they got together and wherever Andy was in the UK, he tried to make it back for this meeting. Many of their prayers and meditations would make their way to the poustinia prayer hut at the Old Bewick church and later into the prayers and meditations of the Northumbrian Office (which later developed into *The Celtic Daily Prayer*).

In 1979, we held our first Easter workshop. It was inspired by one of Andy's friends and was intended to be a series of creativity workshops. Easter workshop became a much-looked-forward-to annual event. A network of relationships developed throughout the old borders of Northumbria and beyond. Kids loved the workshops because they lacked the conventional restraints of church and they were included, without saying, in all the activities. Some of the children began Easter workshops together as babies and toddlers and ended as teens. The formula was simple: hire a church hall somewhere in Northumbria, preferably with support from the host church. Move in for three days, a week or a fortnight. Everybody sleeps on the floor. Cook simple meals. Split into groups to share the chores and the prayers. Leave watches at home. Spend as much time as possible together. Share hopes and dreams, disappointment and loss. Be yourself and share in the workshops.

From the beginning, it was decided to have alternative times for the workshops each year. One year, the workshops would take place over the Easter period, taking in most of the Holy Week. The next year, the workshops would begin before and end on Palm Sunday. The reason was simple: most participants were members of a church. It was unfair to encourage them to be away from their church every Easter, a major festival in the Christian year. However, whatever the venue or the time, the workshops would always conclude on The Holy Island of Lindisfarne, even if only a few could make this final event. This became an essential feature of the Easter workshop.

During Easter Week, there were several activities that became a feature of the workshops. Foot-washing on Maundy Thursday created an opportunity for a year of accumulated difficulties in relationships to be washed away. Folk would just sit around, often drinking coffee, while towels and dishes were made available. Foot-washing was not only a way of saying sorry, it was also a point of contact, a moment of affirmation. Stations of the Cross, the dramatization of Jesus' walk to his execution on the cross, would sometimes take place in public with music and dance serving as the vehicles for telling the story. Whenever possible, tides allowing, all joined in the celebration of the Easter Eucharist at the Parish Church on the Island. A presentation would take place beside the statue of St. Aidan and within the grounds of the Priory. Finally, Easter baptisms took place in the icy cold North Sea followed by a wee dram of whisky for all. Many of the themes that developed at the workshops found their way into the life and language of the Northumbria Community.

Money had always been a problem for Linda and I when we were at college as we both only had small grants towards our tuition and daily living costs. Linda was behind with her college fees and the cost of the new house added to our difficulties. Dour Dougie was given short notice that he and his wife, plus their new baby, had to leave their rented house. He asked if we could put him up. The thought of living in the same house as Dour Dougie, with a mission to convert me, was not very appealing. Linda had other ideas and wanted them to stay. I made an agreement with her. We had no double bed they could use. We agreed that if somebody gave us a bed, then we would take them in. A sure winner for me. That same night there was a knock on the door. It was the Sally Army Captain, "Hi John, do you need a double bed? I have one spare." Dour Dougie and family moved in. They kept themselves private, rarely mixing with us or our visitors and cooking their own meals. They had a two-bar electric fire burning night and day to keep the room warm for Dour Dougie Junior. They were with us for three months. The electric bills were horrendous and they never offered any money to help. Turned out Dour Dougie was also a canny Scot.

Andy was good at saving money rather than sharing it. He never contributed to the household expenses. As well as his room, he also joined in most meals. I did notice that when we were short of cash and food was scarce, he managed to conjure up little treats for himself. Towards the end of his stay, we discovered he had a savings account with a decent amount of cash in it that he had got from his mother. When I challenged him about, his defence was: "This is my trip to the USA money and it can't be touched."

The added costs meant we were robbing Peter to pay Paul. We used to hide from the milkman who would call every Saturday with his bill. Then there was the notice from the electricity people, threatening to cut the supply off. It turned out that my dad did come from a well-to-do family. Mam had been left money in a will of which hundreds of the family were recipients. It wasn't a vast legacy but a very welcome one. She offered to help Linda and I out if we ever needed it. I guess now was the time to take up her offer. I drove down to Jarrow and stayed overnight. In the bedroom was a book of daily readings from the Bible. I turned to the correct date to see what g-d had in store for me. It was a story about a Jew who during a time of famine, went down to Egypt to borrow grain when g-d had told him not to go. As a result, he died in Egypt. Good bedtime reading. The next morning, I was feeling unnerved by the story from the night before. Mam also looked anxious. She explained that she was uneasy about lending me any money, it just didn't feel right, so I jumped in the car and headed back to Berwick, empty handed.

Once home, I was greeted by a barrage of bills, including a hand-written one from the milkman. It was very depressing so much so I nearly left the last official looking letter, afraid it was another demand for money. It was from the Diocese of Durham. They had agreed to contribute to my education and the first instalment was enclosed, a very nice cheque. The milkman was very happy and we were very happy to pay our bills and cover our debts.

Earlier in the year, my friend and mentor David Martineau had gone to see the Bishop of Jarrow and asked him to reconsider sponsoring me for ordination. Linda and I had both been confirmed into the Church of England. I was now about to get the academic qualifications I needed to get into a theological college and I was married with a child. A meeting was set up and Bishop Alexander and I got on great. He agreed to sponsor me and arranged a selection conference to decide if I was suitable for ordination.

It was a three-day event and I was extremely nervous. There are various personal interviews and events led by a selection committee who decide your fate. These include clergy and laity. It turned out my mental health issues were my trump card. Several of the committee had experienced or were in the middle of some mental health issue. I spent most of the conference exchanging stories with these folks and sharing coping mechanisms. I completely forgot the nature of the conference, but was lucky to pass with flying colours. The last obstacle was an interview with a leading psychiatrist to see if my disturbed childhood and traumatic teenage years were going to be a hindrance to my future ministry. The psychiatrist came to the same conclusion as the selection committee: I had used the trauma to grow and develop as a person and gain insight into our human condition. It was now official: I was no longer the disturbed teenager. I had overcome all the obstacles that were in the way of my ordination as a priest in the Church of England. I enjoyed my time at Bible College and made peace with the people of the Megalomaniac. They were not only perpetrators of this evil ideology, but also its victims.

It was time to move on. Lincoln Theological College was beckoning.

3. SEX, SECRETS, SILENCE

Facebook 20/06/2015 21:50
Hi ru the john skinner who was a priest at st clares?

I was going through my evening ritual of checking emails and social media sites when I received this message. I was a little taken aback. One sentence had raised my anxiety levels. My hands were shaking, my mouth dry. I wasn't sure how to reply.

Facebook 20/06/2015 21:55
Yes sir… your name rings a bell

That's all I could think to say. I had no idea what this message was about. I was not keen to open the door to a trauma and injustice I had left behind many moons ago.

Facebook 20/06/2015 22:00
I thnk u shud have a look on the northern echo website.

Extract taken from *The Northern Echo* (18/06/2015, 06:00):
A FORMER minister who held one of the most senior roles in the North-East church is facing trial for a string of serious sex offences dating back to the 1970s.

The Venerable Granville Gibson, 79, former Archdeacon of Auckland, County Durham, appeared at Newton Aycliffe Magistrates Court today charged with eight offences in total, relating to two alleged victims, both of whom were teenagers at the time.

The charges included seven counts of indecent assault and one of buggery on a man aged 16 or over. All of the alleged offences are said to have taken place in Newton Aycliffe and Consett between 1977 and 1983.

I stared at the headline in utter disbelief. Rev Granville Gibson was my boss when I started my first job in the Church of England in 1981. Both Linda and I had been so excited. I had beaten the odds and won my place, becoming a Church of England minister. I had completed my training at

Lincoln Theological College, had been ordained at Durham Cathedral, when only months into the job he tried to sexually assault me, thrusting his erect penis into my leg under the cover of a friendly hug. When I moved away from him, he acted as if nothing had happened. Weeks later, a member of our church and friend of Gibson and his wife asked to see me. She had seen Gibson kissing a young man in the church. This young man was part of the Vietnamese boat people, a vulnerable and homeless group we had agreed to care for in our parish. There were numerous rumours about Gibson and his sexual activity. Several of our young lads joked about never being left alone with him. I feared for them. So, what would you do if you were in my shoes?

I arranged a meeting with Gibson with the intention of confronting him with the allegations made against him and to ask for an explanation for what he had done to me. He denied everything. He had not kissed anyone in church. I had misunderstood his warm embrace for a sexual advance. I was advised, as a junior clergyman, not to listen to parish gossip and get on with my job. I had no idea what to do next. A complaint already had been made against him by another member of the church. Did I have to report him too?

I confided in one of the other priests who was in Gibson's team. He was older and more experienced than me. He advised me NOT to report the incidents to anyone, not least the Bishop. He warned me that they would get rid of me if I reported Gibson. He implored me to be careful who I confided in. He seemed genuinely interested in my welfare, rather than a cover up for Gibson. I was more confused. I felt like I had walked into a world of smoke and mirrors where nothing was as it seemed. This was more alarming than glittering images, you could get badly burnt if you went anywhere near this. I was stuck. I decided to contact my mentor David Martineau.

Then something unexpected happened: Gibson turned up at my door. Linda let him in and he asked to see me. He was highly charged, agitated and emotional. He blurted out that he needed help. He was having affairs with men, both inside and outside of the parish. He was afraid his wife and four children would find out. What if he lost his job? As a priest, you are provided with a house as part of your salary. No job meant no house. I got the impression he had overstepped the mark with someone, hence the danger of getting found out. But why tell me? When he asked me what to do, I suggested he contact a senior clergyman for advice and counselling. I didn't have the experience to help. I encouraged him to get help immediately as he was spiralling out of control. People were going to get hurt. Several days later he turned up at the house again. This time he had his old air of self-confidence and control. He claimed he had seen a senior priest who had cast a demon of homosexuality out of him. He was now ok. What utter nonsense! When I asked who the senior priest was, he said it didn't matter, all was well now and there was no need to take things any further. I had been set up.

After much thought, I decided to report Gibson to John Habgood, Bishop of the Diocese of Durham. The Bishop of a Diocese is essentially the boss. John Habgood lived in the Bishop's Palace at Bishop Auckland, a reminder of the power and prestige that was once enjoyed by the Church of England. For a junior clergyman, going to see the Diocesan Bishop and not his assistant, is a serious affair. I told the Bishop of my own run in with Gibson, his reported liaison in the church; the comments from our young people; Gibson's own admission of having affairs with other men; his fear of being caught; and his deliverance from a "spirit of homosexuality." The Bishop was difficult to read. After I had finished, he politely informed me that he would speak to Gibson directly and then get back to me.

You can imagine the tension that existed between Gibson and I during this time. He did everything to avoid me, including giving me a heavy workload. The Bishop summoned me back to the Palace. This time he did the talking. Gibson denied any knowledge of the incidents I had reported. The Bishop said I had been wrong to listen to parish gossip and that, in future, I needed to be more professional. I asked him what he was going to do about the incident between Gibson and myself. He said I must have misunderstood the situation. What about his admissions of guilt? No reply. I also asked him what response I had to make to the parishioner who had reported Gibson for kissing a vulnerable young man in church. He said that was no longer my business. Was he concerned Gibson may be abusing young men in the parish? No reply. I was given two options: return to the parish and work with Gibson or be moved to the Newcastle Diocese, providing they would have me. That was that: play the game or its over and out.

I took the second option and Linda and I went to Newcastle. The opening sentences from the team vicar (lead priest) were: "Did you not know Gibson was homosexual? Why report him?" When I returned home, Gibson rang me to complain that I had discussed his personal life with the priest in Newcastle. I hadn't. Once again, I was summoned to the Bishop's Palace. The atmosphere was hostile. I explained why I would not move to Newcastle, nor work with Gibson until an investigation had taken place. The Bishop was angry. He said that I had placed myself in an untenable position. I was to give him my church keys, return home and write my letter of resignation to Gibson. I was not to visit any of our churches. If I spoke to anyone about the reasons for my departure or spoke privately or publicly about Gibson, he would use the full force of the Church and take legal action against me. My license to work as a priest was revoked. I was out on my ear.

I left the Bishop's Palace in shock. I had been unsure what to expect, but hadn't anticipated this. What was I going to tell Linda? How was I going to provide for my family? What would I say to our friends and family? What answer would I give to those parishioners who would seek me out and ask why I left? After six years, overcoming the obstacles that were required to become a priest, I was out, shown the door and pushed through it. It was only eighteen months doing the job I loved, the only job I was trained to do. In one afternoon, I lost my house, my salary, my pension, my vocation, my reputation and nearly my mind. I believed the Bishop when he said he would use the full force of the Church against me. I had just got a taste of it. I wrote a very nice letter of resignation, thanking Granville for his support. I couldn't take any more abuse, either from Gibson or the institutional abuse from the mighty Church of England. I had been KO'd, knocked out.

With no money or prospects, Linda and I had no choice but to remain in Newton Aycliffe. Word soon got around that I was no longer at the church. There were lots of telephone calls and visits from former parishioners asking why I had left. A couple I had recently married stopped to ask me if their marriage was still valid. As with every abuser, Gibson fuelled rumours and innuendos about why I had left the church, painting a dark picture of me.

We managed to get a council house on the edge of town. I went to the local unemployment office to sign on. "What kind of job did you say you did Mr Skinner? A priest? Not sure we can help you there, we have no priest jobs on our books." No job and no money coming in spelt trouble. The bank repossessed our car. They then sent bailiffs to see if we had anything else of value. When there was nothing left to take, I was taken to court and ordered to pay a small monthly sum off what I still owed. With court and bailiff fees my debt had now risen considerably. Linda was expecting our third child. I was already worried about her mental health, now I was worried about keeping a roof over our heads.

I got a call from the rent office at the local council. It was to enquire why I hadn't paid my rent. I was asked to pop into the office for a chat. The rent officer transformed my situation. When she heard the circumstances (not all of them) of my departure from the church she put a plan in action to help me. First, she arranged housing benefit. It was backdated so my debt was paid off and from that moment onwards my rent was paid. She advised me to go back to the unemployment office and tell them I was prepared to take any job. As a result, I started receiving unemployment benefit. Some church folk brought bags of food and clothes for the kids. We were overwhelmed by the generosity of many people in the local community.

The Roman Catholic priest, who was very conservative and believed Catholicism and Anglicanism don't mix, asked me to speak at a youth rally organised for Catholic young people. It was an incredible gesture, the meaning of which would not be lost on the Catholic community. Gibson did everything he could to stop me speaking at the event. He rang the priest to try and persuade him to cancel the invitation. He also wrote the first of several letters to the Bishop suggesting I was starting my own church as well as making several other false accusations.

Then there was Michael Prouting, the local Methodist minister. He and I became great friends and he would often ask my advice when faced with people who had come to him for help with mental health issues. He offered to host one of our next Easter workshops. Andy Raine had been living with us in Aycliffe so it seemed a natural progression to say yes to Michael's offer. Once again, Gibson tried to close it down. We ended up having a fantastic week, teaming up with a special needs school who joined in many of our events.

Michael had a church member whose husband wanted to get baptised. Anglicans and Methodists have the tradition of infant baptism so it is rare to baptise an adult. His wife wanted to join him. We discovered she had been baptised as a baby, he had not. That meant Michael could only baptise him. As I was still an Anglican priest, technically I was not allowed to baptise her. Stale mate. Word got out and Gibson organised his assistant priests to visit me. I explained the dilemma and told them I was undecided what to do. According to Gibson I had already baptised a whole host of people who were now part of my new house church. (The House Church Movement was a breakaway group from the C of E. I knew folk in the movement, but disliked what it represented). More letters sent to the Bishop. I decided to go ahead with the baptism. I knew this would close the door to the Church of England. Having disobeyed the Bishop and transgressed Church law, I would need to give up being a priest. This is a legal process where I would be required to sign a Deed of Relinquishment.

It arrived by post. I signed and returned it. I was no longer the Reverend John T. Skinner.

By this time Linda had given birth to Sadie who joined sisters Jayne and Sara, now four and two. The birth was straightforward. What's more, Linda turned a complete corner in her battle with puerperal psychosis and got out of its grip. It would never return. Our dear friends Chris and Sandra Haggerstone who we met in Berwick upon Teed, came to live in Newton Aycliffe. They were joined by Alan and Penny Andrews who moved to be with us from Nuneaton near Coventry. After Sadie's arrival, our GP came to the house to check on how she was doing. During the visit, he kept looking in my direction. He asked if I had been unwell. "Well, kind of." I told him about my raging thirst, my constant peeing, the weight loss and the blurred vision. He rang for an ambulance before telling me he suspected I had type 1 diabetes. Around the same time, I started getting chest pain, especially around anything related to the Church. I wrote it off as a flare up of acid reflux. Five years later, aged 34, I would have my first suspected mild heart attack. I knew from experience, when painful memories are repressed, they come back as symptoms. My GP said type 1 diabetes is often triggered by an emotional trauma. He said he knew Gibson so could imagine what I had been through. It would be difficult to make the link between Gibson and my physical illnesses. However, the link has been made to what happened to me next.

With the arrival of Sadie, Linda's recovery and surrounded by a supportive community, life was looking better. But signing the Deed of Relinquishment was the finale to a terrible ordeal we had suffered at the hands of the Church of England. I call it "institutional abuse." A vortex opened in my psyche, I fell into it and when I landed, it was in a deep, dark place. You don't choose depression, it chooses you, any time, any place. I didn't want to eat or wash. I wanted to be alone, to sleep. I was suicidal. I started to drink again (the lessons learned at Parkwood House kept alcohol in its place and its presence once again at this stage in my life was strangely comforting). Linda and my friends were worried about me. A decision was made to contact our dear friends John and Marg Patterson.

They came to see me. I was in a bad way and was open to any ideas they had. They asked me to stand up. John laid his hands on my head. After a few minutes, unconditional love turned up. As I gently fell backwards, Marg caught me and gently laid me on the floor. After several minutes John asked how I felt. I was very calm, resting, peaceful, safe, floating. He then asked where I was. It was a very dark place not a psychic darkness, but simply a place with no light. It felt like a confined space, perhaps a small room or some other small space. I could hear people talking outside of the space that I was in. The words were mumbled, unclear. I felt I could hear the emotion that was conveyed in the words, not audibly, but with another sense, as if my inner spirit or soul had the ability to hear feelings. There was anger, conflict and anxiety, followed by disappointment, despair and despondency.

I heard myself repeating over again, "It's all your fault. It's all your fault. It's all your fault." I was subdued, but settled back into my safe place. I didn't want to leave here ever. I was the cause of all the negative emotions. Whatever I had done, must have been bad. I wanted to sleep. John asked me not to go to sleep, but to stay in the moment. Suddenly, I felt disorientated, light headed, woozy. At the same time, I felt as if my skin was burning. Yet there was no pain, no physical pain, no emotional pain just a numb feeling. In my safe space, this comforted me. Then, sometime later, a door opened, the light came and I was in a much bigger space. There were people greeting me, holding me. I felt numb, empty. Once again, I could hear myself speaking, "It's too late now, I know what you did. It's too late now, I know what you did." Then it was over.

We were all emotionally exhausted when it ended. We sat in silence drinking endless cups of tea and coffee. Something had just happened. What had happened? I had no idea. John had written it all down. He handed me the paper. He encouraged me that the meaning of what we had experienced would unravel in the coming weeks. He was right.

I discovered Mam was unwell. She had a progressive illness. Not only did her joints dry up and break, her neck often froze in one position. Her tear ducts dried up too and she was unable to cry. I decided to go and see her. On the way to Jarrow I had an uneasy feeling she was going to tell me her secret. I sat on her bed and drank tea. Unable to move her neck, she sat facing forward. I had brought some oil that I used to anoint the sick. I stood over her and prayed, then sat back on the bed. She turned her head towards me, "We were going to abort you." She then proceeded to cry a bucketful of tears as I cradled her broken body in my arms. I wept with her and for her. Poor Mam, so much to carry in a lifetime. She told me the story. First, they had little money. Dad had persuaded her to have two abortions after Alan was born. The doctor had agreed to do them because he was afraid that her next baby would be too big for her to give birth safely. When she got pregnant with me, she and dad argued over the need for another abortion. She put her foot down this time and refused. Mam had saved my life. There it was, the secret was out. Or was it?

Back in Aycliffe, life continued. Brenda Grace, who was part of our small community, offered Alan and I a room in her house for an art studio and a place to study. Alan Andrews was a gifted graphic designer and he began two new series of painting with wooden blocks. One was called *Internal Emigres*, the second *Winter Night*. These were reflections on the academic work I was undertaking regarding the post-Christian society and Bonhoeffer's new type of monasticism. These themes would provide the language, metaphors and symbols for the emerging Northumbria Community. It was now two years since my exit from the Church of England. I had a strong sense of wanting to return to Northumberland. I shared it with our community. Although all felt it was the right move, it was upsetting to think about a separation. Chris and Sandra decided to move with us. Brenda Grace would join us later. For Alan and Penny and the rest of the crew it was a step too far.

Linda had given birth to Benjamin David, the last of our tribe. Chris and Sandra had two girls and one boy all around the same age. Every Monday, we would meet and get out an ordinance survey map of Northumberland. We created a triangle using Holy Island, Alnmouth Friary and Shepherd's Law Hermitage as our points of reference. Our new home or homes were somewhere in that triangle. Over the next six months, we would regularly use our family allowances to hire a mini bus. We would load the kids in and drive the length and breadth of the triangle looking for a house. Chris and I also went camping and walking in the area. After six months, I lost confidence in the move. Chris had one of his mystical moments and announced that we would be moving to Glanton. I had a chuckle. Undeterred, he started looking for jobs and a house in that area. He applied for a job collecting eggs with a cottage thrown in. He didn't tell me about it.

Days later, Linda announced that we had a house. "That's great, where is it?" I replied. She had no idea, but was convinced we would hear soon. Chris got a reply to his application, had an interview, then announced he had a job and a house in Glanton. One of our friends Norma Wise sent us a message to get in touch with John Ferguson. John and I were at theological college together and he was now working in a parish in Northumberland. A few months earlier, he had asked for my advice and support in a personal matter. As a thank you, he asked if I needed anything. "Yes," I joked, "a house in Northumberland." John rang me. "Hi John. Guess what? I have got you a house in Northumberland. It's at Glanton." I was properly stunned. Turned out it was a wing of the former Dowager house on the Ravensworth Estate. Synchronicity and g-d were at work again.

Before leaving, I decided to go and see Auntie Freda. She was married to Eddy and during my wild teenage years they had been my rock. Like Freda, Eddy was disabled too. He was also fiercely independent and drove a specially adapted mini to his workplace. Having lived at home with Nana and Granda until she married in her thirties, Auntie was unofficially the family memory and secret keeper. I was agitated by Mam's confession. Auntie knew there were deep tensions between me and Mother. A few years earlier, when things were bad, she told me Mam had been sexually abused by a close family member. Good job Granda didn't find out, he would have sorted him out! It did make me see Mam in a new way and explained how she could exit her body in the middle of a trauma. It didn't change my opinion about Mother. I took a deep breath and jumped in with my rehearsed comment:

"Mam told me about the abortion."

"I am glad she told you, she has been carrying the guilt for years. She should never have done it."

"Oh my g-d! What did she do?" My head was spinning. This was the dark secret and I was about to hear it.

"I told her it wouldn't work, gin and a hot bath are not going to do away with a baby. That's just an old wives' tale."

She then went on to tell the story. Yes, Mam had two abortions after Alan. Both were unplanned pregnancies and with money already short, they felt they could not support another child. Alan had been a big baby so the family doctor agreed to both abortions because of the possible dangers. When they applied for my abortion, the doctor said no.

I tried to stay calm, but my heart was beating fast. I had a dull pain in my chest and my breathing was short and laboured. I thanked Auntie and headed for the car to drive back to Aycliffe. My mind was racing. I had to stop at the side of the road because I thought I was going to pass out. Auntie wasn't sure if Mam had gone ahead with her gin and bath. They never talked about it again. I was sure she did. The experience I had when John and Marg prayed for me confirms the gin and bath story. It could also explain my strange relationship with alcohol. So many pieces of the jigsaw were falling into place and I wasn't happy at the picture I was seeing. Mam had lied to me, she wasn't the hero in the story. She had tried to get the doctor to abort me and, now, it seems likely she tried to abort me herself. I have always coped with the dark side of Mam by calling her Mother. Now I had to come to terms with the fact that Mam and Mother were the same person. I was gutted. I would need some time to get my head around that. For the moment, I needed to get back to Linda and the kids, the only stable points in my life. It was time to return to Northumberland.

First, to the unfinished business of institutional abuse by the Church of England. It turned out that the person who messaged me on Facebook with information about Gibson was one of his victims. When he told his parents what was happening, they refused to believe him. As a result, he ended up in care. Gibson had messed not only with his body, but also his head. He never recovered from the abuse and his mam and dad died still not believing him.

I contacted Darlington police and offered to make a statement. We were living in Turkey at the time so it was agreed that I would be interviewed on a Skype call. It was all a little nerve racking, but the police officers were great, professional and friendly at the same time. My evidence was going to prove crucial to the case. I received an email from the child protection officer in the Durham Diocese offering help and support. I thought it hilarious. How ironic that after all these years, all the institutional abuse, somebody now cares! The Bishop of Durham responded to Gibson's arrest and charges with the usual institutional soundbites:

Extract taken from *The Guardian* (Thursday 4th August 2016):

Responding to the verdict, Paul Butler, the present bishop of Durham and until recently the C of E's lead bishop on safeguarding, said: "We offer an unreserved apology to all the survivors and those affected by this news. We commend the bravery of those who brought these allegations forward, acknowledging how difficult and distressing this would have been.

"We are profoundly sorry for the abuse perpetrated by Mr Gibson and remain committed to doing everything possible to ensure the wellbeing of children, young people and adults, who look to us for respect and care. Abuse is a terrible crime and a grievous breach of trust, which has lifelong effects."

Butler said he had ordered an independent review of the circumstances surrounding the case.

Sounds great, doesn't it? But the reality is something else. I got my letter from the Bishop, apologising for Gibson's abuse and the promise of: "You are in my prayers." I found the piety nauseating. There was no mention of or apology for the institutional abuse visited upon my family.

In preparation for the legal case, I wrote to the Diocese of Durham and requested my personal file that records my history within the Diocese. I was surprised by the size and details it contained: every letter exchanged, every meeting recorded in detail. From my earliest contact with Bishop Alexander Hamilton to the relinquishment of my religious orders, all detailed. Yet there were no records relating to my meetings and correspondence with Bishop John Habgood regarding Granville Gibson. Either it had never been recorded or, most likely, it had been removed. Furthermore, my records after I reported Gibson were deliberately arranged to look like I had returned to being the disturbed teenager and was now deliberately causing trouble in the parish. I found it all deeply distressing. I wrote to Paul Butler, the current Bishop of Durham, expressing my distress and concern about the missing records and the amended narrative to paint me in a bad light. This was his reply:

Dear John,

I am not surprised that you find it distressing to hear that there are no records of the meetings to which you refer from the early 1980s. I find it deeply distressing too.

If notes were made then they have clearly been removed or destroyed at some point before 2008 when the review of files was done.

However, John Habgood now has serious dementia so there is no hope of discovering anything from him directly. It is almost certain that we will not be able to discover when these records were removed or destroyed.

Hence the question to you about whether or not you have any record yourself so that at least those could be copied and placed in the file.

Please be assured that we have cooperated with every request made to us by the police as they have pursued their investigations.

I can only apologise deeply on behalf of the church that these important records were at some point removed from your file.

Yours sincerely
+Paul

The Crown Court Case against Gibson began on the 25th July 2016. Gibson pleaded not guilty to all charges, which meant it was the abused not the abuser who went on trial. Gibson's barrister was brutal. The man who messaged me had his testimony destroyed. He was painted as a needy and disturbed child who had lied about Gibson. This was exactly how his parents had reacted to him when he told them about Gibson's abuse. Can you imagine how he felt standing in court, years later and getting the same response? His case was not proven because the jury could not agree if Gibson was guilty or not. He was and remains devastated. The next victim was stronger. He had reported Gibson and had waited years for justice.

The barrister took a different tack with me: it was more innuendo than direct attack. He read out my very polite resignation letter to Gibson to the jury. I reminded him that it was written soon after Bishop John Habgood had forced my resignation and threatened me with legal action if I said anything derogatory about Gibson. He finished by extolling the many titles and academic qualifications of Baron John Habgood QC and asked why he would conduct himself in the manner I had described. I said I could not speak for Bishop Habgood but what we had learned in our society was that aristocratic, religious titles, academic qualifications and professional honours do not guarantee the moral character of a person.

Extract taken from *The Guardian* (Thursday 4th August 2016):

A senior Church of England clergyman has been found guilty of sex offences committed against two young men in the 1970s and 80s amid claims of a church cover-up.

A jury at Durham crown court found George Granville Gibson, 80, the former archdeacon of Auckland, guilty of two counts of indecent assault against two men, then aged 18 and 26. He was found not guilty of buggery and four other charges of indecent assault. Two charges of indecent assault were dropped.

It was a poor result, especially for the victims who were left in no man's land and sentenced to more years of heartache. I think the truth has not yet been fully revealed and more victims will come forward. It is often said that people were less aware in my day of the dangers of sexual exploitation and there were not the laws to protect people. This suggests that because today we are more aware of the risks of sexual abuse and exploitation that we now have enough safeguards to significantly reduce the number of victims. In truth, sexual exploitation, especially of young children is on the rise in these so called enlightened times and the perpetrators include those at the very heights of the establishment. Yet the motivation to cover up these foul crimes is still actively at work both in the church and other institutions.

My lawyer is currently negotiating financial compensation with the Diocesan insurance company. Claims against the Church for sexual abuse are small and certainly don't hurt, so don't encourage change. We need something that hurts to counter the institutional abuse and violence that the Church aims at victims and whistle blowers who report sexual abuse. I want it to stop. As a result, I have joined a group that is committed to making it a criminal offence NOT to report knowledge of sexual abuse and to have it applied to historic cases. If that was on the statute book today, then the last three Archbishops of York and one Archbishop of Canterbury would be investigated regarding this law and could be prosecuted. When church officials do not report abuse, then the abusers go on abusing. More people are hurt and injured because of the silence of those who should speak. In my mind, if you do not report abuse, then you share the responsibility for the abuser's crimes and should be prosecuted accordingly.

4. DISTANCE, DIMINISH, DELETE

In 2009, Linda and I returned to Hetton Hall, home to the Northumbria Community. The Community were packing up and getting ready to move to a new location. This was the first time we had been back to Hetton Hall since the traumatic break with the Community ten years earlier. We were apprehensive and nervous about "coming home."

Linda and I had given over twenty years to founding, nurturing and caring for the Northumbria Community. We brought up our four kids in the middle of the hardships, struggles and tensions that exist in an emerging community. In return, we experienced that deep sense of belonging that happens when people are thrown together by the need to find new meaning for their lives.

We pulled up at the front door, took a deep breath, got out of the car and knocked on the door. We were greeted by a couple who were on the staff at Hetton Hall (the Hall acts as the hub for the Community which is international with a dispersed membership). Those first moments were tense and awkward. The real reasons for the traumatic break with the Community have never been made public. Community members, both past and present, must be content with the rumours and innuendos that have been circulating since we left or the fact there is no mention of us at all. We fully understood the caution that the staff demonstrated when we first met and the hesitancy in their body language. It was like they were meeting the family ghosts and they did not know if we were harmless or terrifying. Once the greeting was over, we were left on our own to wander the house and grounds to reminisce. The first and overall impression was: nothing had changed, pretty much everything was just the same as when we had left.

We wandered around the house and gardens and looked through the windows of the old stable block, which we had renovated to use as our family home. We sat in the chapel that had been built out of rough wood by members and friends of the Community. It was a surreal experience. On the one hand, we were reliving great memories of the people and events that had shaped the very soul of the Community. On the other hand, it was as if time had stood still. We were trapped in a time warp, suffocating, sinking and needing air.

We discovered that there was a photograph collection on the dining room notice board: a celebration of the people, events and memories of the Community's time at Hetton Hall. We decided to take a look. We recognised all of the faces in the photographs, so many dear people who had contributed to the welcoming ethos that was a defining characteristic of the Community. There wasn't a single photograph of Linda, me or the kids. We went to the office to look at the other photographs included in the celebration. Guess what? You guessed right. Same position, there wasn't a single photograph of myself, Linda or our family. It was as if we were never part of the story, as if we had never existed. Ironically, the hall, the stable block, the chapel, the gardens, and the Community itself are the very evidence of our history there. We had organised all the renovations, tended to the gardens and led the growing Community. Sadly, someone had reached right into the heart of the Community and pulled out any memories associated with us.

As soon as Linda and I had been ousted from the Community, a plan had been put in place to ensure that a distance was created between the Community and us. As the distance grew, our contribution to the vision and vocation of the Community (which had been foundational, wide-ranging and significant) was severely diminished until we were deleted out of the narrative.

Not only Linda and I were stripped of our history, so was the Northumbria Community. For a community to thrive and continue to evolve, it must be connected to its history. Memories create the language and traditions in a community that nurture its life and ethos. Distance, diminish and delete the memories and a community will continue for a time, living off the legacy of its founders. Eventually, it will evolve into a very different creature to what was originally intended or, more likely, just come to an end.

For those reasons, I would like my history and my work back so I can continue to contribute to the ongoing new monasticism event. I would also like the members of the Northumbria Community to get their history back so they can decide for themselves how to move forwards into a new day and not have the future dictated to them.

In 1995, I had informed the trustees that I wanted to stand down from leading the Community and to pursue the work we had begun in Ephesus,

Turkey. Following that meeting, the chairman of the trustees asked to have a word. He was concerned that Roy Searle and Trevor Miller were not ready to take over my responsibilities. He also felt that we should put more infrastructure in place to support the growth in membership. He asked if I would stay on for another two years. To be honest, I would have preferred to leave sooner rather than later but agreed to his request. I didn't know then the size of the task I was taking on. During the additional two years, it was agreed that a new trust would be set up to support our mission in Europe, from Turkey to Ireland. I would oversee the European work, located in Turkey at a base in Ephesus. The new trust would provide the financial support required to kick start the new work, including financial support for Linda, myself and our family.

My first move was to present a paper to the leaders, trustees and directors of our community business. It was a reflection on the most important moments in the history of the Community to date and a proposal to reform the Community Council. I felt it was important to remind ourselves of where we had come from in the face of significant change and new opportunities. The paper I prepared was called "THE CALL TO COMMUNITY: from the founders, to the few, to the many." This paper covers a period of sixteen years and identifies some of the key events in the emergence of the Northumbria Community.

(The text in italics and/or bold are taken directly from the original paper).

THE CALL TO COMMUNITY
From the founders, to the few, to the many

Our main challenge this year is to share the responsibility and liability for the vision, administration and care of the Northumbria Community.

This opening paragraph outlines the intention of the paper, which was to reform the Community Council so it would be able to lead the Community into the future.

INTRODUCTION
During the January retreat, we have been outlining significant periods in the life of the community.

1. Founders   1979 - 1990
Andy Raine, John & Linda Skinner.

During this period came:

- The vision of the Upper & Nether Springs;
- A lifelong commitment to Holy Island;
- Easter workshops;
- All the foundational aspects of the Rule;
- A commitment to find and establish the place of the Nether Springs;
- The Grange, the first place of the Nether Springs.

1979 – 1990 are the most significant years in the foundation and emergence of the Northumbria Community. Yet these are the "missing years" from the history of the Community and they need to be returned.

Upper Springs

Storytelling had a special place in the emerging community. The use of metaphors, images and models were key to focusing attention on the direction that we began to take on this daily, unfolding journey. They were also essential for organising meaning around subjects and events that were complex and yet to be fully understood, if they ever could be. An example of this are the metaphors "the upper and nether springs." They were originally used in a Bible verse in the Old Testament:

> She replied, "Do me a special favor. Since you have given me land in the Negev, give me also springs of water." So Caleb gave her the upper and lower springs (Joshua 15:19 NIV).

Andy Raine moved in with us in 1979, during our time at Bible College. He had conveyed to us the significance of the Holy Island of Lindisfarne, which was a few miles south of Berwick-upon-Tweed. Holy Island was the epicentre of Irish/Celtic monasticism. It was to here in 625 AD that St Aidan, an Irish Monk, travelled from St. Columba's monastery on the Isle of Iona, off the west coast of Scotland. He came at the request of the Northumbrian King Oswald who was based nearby at Bamburgh. Aidan established a monastery on Holy Island which consisted of a wooden enclosure, the huts the monks lived in, a refectory and the wooden church. Irish/Celtic Christianity had monasticism at its heart and was an altogether different species to European Christianity. Irish Christianity would have a defining influence on the ethos of the Northumbria Community. Geography, the significance of place, was important to the Celts, as it became to us.

The ebb and flow of the Holy Island tides captured the ethos of the

Irish Church. As a monastic community, the hut or cell was the centre of their lives. They were like hermits in a community, coming together to eat, for worship on Sundays and to share stories and music. As the tide was going out, they would often leave with it. The sea and her tributaries were the motorways and A roads of the period, taking them to new places and to new people. When the monks had become experienced, they were kicked out the monastery. They were told to keep walking until they found the place and people they were to settle among. This was the place they would live out their lives and be at one with the people who lived there. They called this "white martyrdom," to be separated from all you love and settle on a foreign shore. They also had "green martyrdom," to spend a life time overcoming the dark desires that are humanity's lot. "Red martyrdom" was to suffer a violent death because of one's faith. Upper springs is not just a geographical location, it speaks of the mission of the Community. The ebb and flow of the fast-moving tides invites us to go and share the sacred anarchy of unconditional love, g-d is with us. We identified Holy Island as the place of the Upper springs.

A lifelong commitment to Holy Island

Andy felt Holy Island was the place where he should settle; life would become defined by that choice. His first move to Holy Island didn't work out: his spiritual advisor Brother Roland Walls suggested he leave for a time. Living with us in Berwick, then Newton Aycliffe, and Glanton was Andy waiting to get the nod from Br. Roland Walls to return. Andy did get back to Holy Island. He is still there today with his wife Anna and their grown-up kids Joel and Martha. To date, the Community has carried on with Easter workshops and its lifelong commitment to Holy Island.

Easter Workshops

I think there were 4 or 5 of us at the first Easter workshop in 1979, then each year, they began to grow. As I said earlier, the format was simple: hire a church hall, bring a sleeping bag, chip in to buy food, join in with whatever activities popped up. The Alnwick Prayer Group were at the heart of the early workshops; some of my best memories are associated with the folk from that group. Having lived all their lives in a deprived area, they were a forgotten people with few resources. Andy had woken a deep creativity in many people, which could be expressed and shared at any level.

I remember one of their first productions, a dance drama. It was widely publicised and there was a good turnout. Folk came from the college, including Roy Searle and my mate Eddie. It was interesting. Andy spent most of the evening helping people to remember their lines or their dance moves. Some great moments and some lows. Roy and Eddie left mid-way through the performance. They told me later it was embarrassing. They missed the point. There were folk in the show who could neither read or write. Two people had special needs. The rest had never done anything like this before. Why would they? Who would be interested? Andy beamed all the way through. I liked him for that.

Groups from Edinburgh, Leicester and Aycliffe joined us and the kids looked forward to Easter more than Christmas. They got to hang out with their friends and to join in with everything. Each year, we would have a theme we would explore. For example, "I am among you as one who serves," an allusion to the time Jesus washed his disciples' feet. We used that theme to encourage folk to leave their religious identities behind so when they joined a workshop, they could get to know other people and not push their own views and beliefs. What we learned together from the workshop themes would become ongoing features of our lives together. The workshops were the sign of an emerging community, not yet ready to reveal itself.

All the foundational aspects of the Rule

A Rule is a body of experience that a community acquires when they are working out how to live their lives together. It is not a set of regulations that someone must police. In 1985, when we all moved to Glanton, we were faced with the fundamental question: how then shall we live? The question at the heart of all communities.

The pressing question when we arrived in Glanton was related to work: what kind of jobs are available? Sandra and Chris got their house with a job collecting eggs. Chris would need to get additional work to pay for a car to take the kids to school and other family necessities. He is multi-practical so started a handyman's business. I had no idea what to do. Linda had a full-time job with our four kids. Andy Robertson, a local man, offered me the window cleaning round he had built up, for free. This included customers and equipment. I was terrified of heights. As a child, I had repeated dreams about climbing onto a ladder and falling off.

Many of Andy's clients had large country houses. There is one incident that was terrifying at the time but hilarious to look back on. I was at a house where you had to climb a ladder to the first floor, then cross a roof to clean windows at the side of the second floor. One morning I slid down the roof and over the eaves of the first-floor roof and was hanging over the edge,

63

clinging onto a gutter pipe. The lady of the house who was enjoying a morning cocktail came out. "Darling," she said, "What are you doing?" "Actually, I'm falling off your roof!" I replied. "My dear, hang on while I change my carpet slippers." A few minutes later, she came out, manoeuvred the ladder to where I was and I climbed down. Two more falls led me to quit.

Chris and I joined forces and began landscape gardening. For one job, we had to hire a JCB, a big mechanical digger. It arrived on site the same day as a business executive arrived at the house, in the middle of a nervous breakdown. A dilemma: I was the only one who could drive the JCB. It was an expensive hire yet the guy had come to see me. What should I do?

A book that really helped us sort out what new monasticism might look like and how to respond to this dilemma was *The Wisdom of the Desert* (1960) by Thomas Merton. It was a book of sayings and stories from men and women who had left their everyday lives to find a different way to live (this was in the 3rd century). In the stories, they send themselves up as they struggle with the complexity of human nature in their new life. For example, they would give pebbles to gossips who had to put them in their mouths until they learned to stop bad-mouthing other people.

Many of the stories are associated with work. They did various things including making baskets, an essential commodity in their day; working for local farmers; weaving linen, which was collected by traders for export. They recognised the need for work, but they emphasised that work was just a part of the life they lived. They were not following a career but doing work, which was an essential part of their vocation. This kept them rooted in ordinary, everyday life and didn't allow them to become vain, religious introverts. They also stressed that being available to other people was the single most important aspect of their lives. If someone knocked on your door, you dropped what you were doing to see what they needed. With those thoughts in mind, it was a no brainer for Chris and I. We left the JCB on site and went to be there for our guest. I spent a week with him. The day the JCB was to be returned, unused, the company rang me up. Could we keep it a few more days at no additional cost? Their transporter had broken down. Thank you very much!

When we arrived in Glanton, I was advised by the Archdeacon of Northumberland that I was not welcome at any of their churches. Furthermore, I was not to impersonate a Church of England minister or I would be prosecuted. "Here we go again," I thought. No church, what happens next? We had tried out a set of prayers that we had prepared at an

Easter workshop. They were said morning, noon and night. Linda is the contemplative and was intent on ensuring that a regular daily discipline of prayer and readings took place for those who were home. Andy Raine was back with us now. He was living in a cupboard in the girl's bedroom. It was only five feet, eight inches wide and Andy is over six foot. Good job he sleeps in the foetal position. Andy had a book of readings and prayers that had been used and collected by the Alnwick folk and at Easter workshops (when the poustinia prayer hut was put up at Old Bewick Church with a bed and seat for the pilgrims, these prayers were available in an exercise book). As the years at The Grange progressed, they were filled with a daily discipline of prayers and readings. Linda used a bell to announce the start of morning, midday and evening prayer and Andy took out the prayer pot, from which three names were pulled to be remembered that day.

Although the prayers (Daily Office) provide a rhythm for the day, their essential purpose is to provide an anchor during a psyche storm. Any major change in life can cause a psyche meltdown. It's well documented that moving house, the birth of a child or a change in your financial position can put you under considerable stress. In our case, we had a lifestyle change forced upon us and we were still in the process of working through that, as well as the new challenges we now faced. The Daily Office provided us with stability when everything was constantly changing around us.

When the Northumbria Community eventually emerged, The Way for Living (Rule) and the Daily Office (Celtic Daily Prayer) provided the means for many more people to test their vocation. As you can see Andy, Linda and I didn't simply sit down one day and create them. They were the fruit of fourteen years of struggle and challenges, joy and pain and plain everyday living.

A commitment to find and establish the place of the Nether Springs

Getting kicked out of the Church in 1984 for whistle blowing on a sexual predator gave me the push I needed to start looking for the place of the Nether Springs and unpacking Bonhoeffer's new type of monasticism.

Starting in 1985, every Monday morning when we sat looking over the ordinance survey map of north Northumberland, Linda, Chris, Sandra and I were looking for the place of the Nether Springs. It would be a place where we could reflect on the loss of belief and religious faith that was taking place in and all around us. It would be a safe place where people could express doubt, recover from abuse and get their heads together. All would be welcome, wherever they came from.

My mentor Brother Roland Walls began a small community on a very posh street in Rosslyn near Edinburgh in Scotland. He and Brother John bought an old tin Nissen hut, a prefabricated temporary structure often used as meeting rooms for coal miners. They used the Nissen hut for their sitting room/library, a couple of guest rooms, kitchen, bathroom and Br Roland's study. In the back garden, they had a big wooden hut that they used as a chapel. The brothers slept in six feet by six feet wooden huts.

A friend of theirs asked if they could take a man for a while who was recovering from a bad mental breakdown. Br. Roland told him that his friend, who was used to many creature comforts, would hate being with them, "Damp rooms and bed linen not dried properly, he will hate it." The man replied, "No, I have been told by the psychologist that what he needs is a place where people failed." He went on, "Yours is the only place I can think of." We wanted the Nether Springs to be just like Br. Roland's place: nobody would ever be intimidated by success, nor made to feel unwelcome and out of place.

The Grange, the first place of the Nether Springs

When we went to see The Grange at Glanton, the first place of the Nether Springs, there were four parts to it and we had the south-facing-wing of the house, on the lower floor. It had two big reception rooms, a good-sized kitchen with a shared yard at the rear and three good-sized bedrooms. There was a rather dilapidated orangery just off the dining room, which became home to our two black Labradors Bo and Duke. We had the sole use of the substantial front garden, which consisted of a very large lawn with a long stone wall called "a ha-ha". It's designed so that you can't see it from the house, giving you a panoramic view over the countryside. On the other side of the wall, adjacent to the farm field, the wall is exposed with a deep ditch. This stops the animals getting in the garden. I twice stepped backwards off that wall when mowing the grass! There was an overgrown vegetable garden, which we turned into a field of flowers. I have already outlined the type of days we had at The Grange earlier in the chapter.

To finish off this section, I want to mention two sets of amazing people. During our time at The Grange, we had two guardian angels in the shape of Norma and Ken Wise. They were members of our old parish in Newton Aycliffe and had stuck with us during that difficult time. They made frequent trips to Glanton with bags of shopping, clothes for the kids, and even condoms (Norma was always practical!) She used to cut the kids' hair and Ken helped with odd jobs. They literally kept us going during those times when we wanted to give up; without them we would have not survived.

The Friars of the Society of Saint Francis (SSF) at Alnmouth really took us to heart. During my time at Berwick, Brother Jonathan the guardian at SSF, became a mentor. He was a gentle and sweet man. Jonathan was gay and carried that deep pain of unrequited love. He used to swim every day, leaving his clothes on the shore. One day he never returned. I and many others were gutted. When we were at The Grange, Brother Colin Wilfred was the guardian. He gave us an amazing oak dining table that became the symbol of hospitality at The Grange. I bet Brother Harry a fiver that it would go in the back of my estate car. We did it. Brother Harry still owes me a fiver.

During one visit, there was a joint communion service led by the Bishop of Newcastle. He invited all the clergy present and the friars to stand close. Despite the obvious hostility from the clergy towards me, Br. Wilfred was having none of it. He came and stood by me. This was an action I will never forget and will always be grateful for. Br. Wilfred was also gay. I am telling you this because in his defence, Gibson hid behind his claim that he was a closet homosexual when in fact he was a serial sexual predator. It should never be assumed for one minute that gay people are paedophiles or sexual predators. That is a travesty of the truth.

In 1990, the last year at The Grange, visitors began to grow, yet work began to suffer and debts began to pile up. Our friends suggested that a charitable trust be set up to raise money for our work. The Nether Springs Trust was born. But it was too late: by the middle of the final year, Linda and I had debts of around £5,000 accumulated over our seven years there. Our electricity was disconnected, we had no coal to heat the house, no hot water and we were feeding the kids donuts at every meal from a huge catering pack we had been given. We were at the end.

Trevor sent me a message with some details of a woman he had met and talked to about my work helping people with mental health issues. I had to walk to the phone box to ring her and reverse the charges. She wanted to give me money for my work. I said I didn't take money from anyone, but my trust would be happy to receive a gift. She insisted the money was for me, no one else. Finally, I agreed. She asked if I wanted to know how much money it was… £23,000! I ran all the way home. Linda would be relieved. By the time I ran a ten-minute mile, I had the money spent: debts paid off, new car, holiday, party and money in the bank for a rainy day!

Linda had a different view: we should give all the money to the new trust. What about our debt? No. What about a new car? No. What about the holiday, party, saving a little? No. When the money arrived, I reluctantly gave it over to The Nether Springs Trust.

At the next trustees' meeting, the normally nervous attitude was so different. When we had no money, shoulders would be slumped and suggestions of how we should proceed were in short supply. Money empowers. Everyone was wanting to get their views over. I was asked to leave the room while they had a discussion. When I returned they had voted and agreed to pay my debt off. The condition was that I didn't get into debt again. I was silent but smiling inside. I was in debt from propping a work up, not because of being reckless. I gave up the money given to me, with no thank you. I made a mental note. Money creates attitude. I knew tougher times were ahead and so it was important our trustees enjoyed this moment.

2. The Few (1990- 1995)
Members of the Nether Springs Trust
Roy & Shirley Searle
Northumbria Ministries

During this period came:
- *A definite move from the founders to the few;*
- *Shared decisions;*
- *A specific commitment to Northumbria;*
- *The establishment of Hetton Hall as the place of the Nether Springs;*
- *The formation of the Northumbria Community;*
- *The beginning of community trading;*
- *The publication of the Office book;*
- *An emerging vision for European mission.*

When I was kicked out of the Church in Aycliffe in 1983, I began keeping journals, records and reflections on my daily lot. I kept up this practice until 1999. My reflections on my paper "THE CALL TO COMMUNITY: from the founders, to the few, to the many" are not something I am doing retrospectively, with hindsight. I am reflecting on each moment through the pages of my journals, on what I was thinking when the events were taking place.

The last year at The Grange was not only busy with people seeking help or advice, we also had a steady flow of people wanting to connect with us. These were always men who were building their networks ("Apostles" they called themselves) and wanted you to join them. No, thank you very much.

Linda and Shirley Searle had kept in touch at Christmas with cards. One year, Linda stuck in a prayer letter and Roy ended up getting in touch. He wanted to arrange a meeting between Andy and I, and his colleagues Jane and Andy Fitzgibbon and their network Northumbria Ministries. I talked about new monasticism and Andy Raine talked about Celtic spirituality. You could see Jane and Andy were uncomfortable throughout the meeting. They wanted nothing to do with us, which is always fine by me. Roy contacted us again. He wanted to take the conversation further and look at getting connected. Andy and Jane had appeared to have fallen off the map.

A definite move from the founders to the few

Roy wanted to join us but was completely unaware of the dilemma I had been trying to solve for several weeks. When we started to answer the monastic conundrum (how then shall we live?) our mentors had been Brother Roland Walls and the monastic communities in Merton's *Wisdom of the Desert* (1960). To really experience their ethos, we had to follow the way they lived: no career, only vocation; no ownership of property; no hanging onto money; no pensions; daily disciplines. You get my meaning. As more property owning, career-minded, savers and security-conscious people joined us, was it possible to translate the essence of monasticism to inform their lifestyles? Had we got too close to traditional monasticism? Monasticism is unintentional. It disrupts, is uncontrollable, unpredictable and dislocates you from your current way of life. It demands your availability and, as a result, plunges you into vulnerability. You don't choose this way for living, it chooses you. An intentional way of living is something you choose, maintain and control. There are few demands because you are calling the shots.

Roy lived in the intentional world. He had not experienced the hardship and heartaches that had given birth to the Community Rule or our way for living, of availability and vulnerability. He would need a lot of mentoring and a willingness to experience the acute tensions that exist between unintentional and intentional living. If he could not make that move, then the danger would be that we would have two ways of living together: the intentional and unintentional. If that happened, then the intentional would win because it appeals to the human need for security. Was I prepared to take that risk? If he was to succeed as an apostle of new monasticism, then he had to experience the tension, the disruption and dislocation of an unconditional way for living. The problem is, I knew Roy would not go to that place easily. The question was: would he go at all? I was going to have to face the problem of how you introduce new people to new monasticism and introduce them to the tensions inherent in the way for living. Did I want to spend the next three years mentoring Roy? Was he the right person in which to invest my time and energy? Would he be able to overcome his unbridled ambition? At the time, I felt I had no choice and that I had to take the risk. We agreed that he could join us.

Shared decisions

After that decision was made, things began to move forward very quickly. The trustees of the Nether Springs Trust and some of the leading people from Northumbria Ministries started to connect. There were some tensions at the beginning as trust is built over time, not over night. Inevitably, the new relationship was not everyone's cup of tea and I started to guess who might drop out. As we started to grow closer, the burden of decision making was spread across the new alliance. It certainly felt lighter for me.

A specific commitment to Northumbria

"Covenanted together in the love of Jesus, we are a group of Christian friends who share a common vision and concern to see God's Kingdom extended in the area covered by the ancient Kingdom of Northumbria, from the Forth to the Humber." Northumbria Ministries

In the 6C AD, the ancient kingdom of Northumbria stretched from the Forth River near Edinburgh to the Humber near Hull. This was the golden age for Irish/Celtic Christianity before the Synod of Whitby in 664 AD when the European Church effectively diminished the Irish Church's position in the UK and Europe. As a result, most Irish monks returned to Ireland or went to other parts of Europe and started monasteries. This did not halt their decline, which proved to be terminal. What we did have in common with Northumbria Ministries was the conviction that Irish/Celtic monasticism has an important contribution to make to the European Church, today in decline itself.

The establishment of Hetton Hall as the place of the Nether Springs

We began to search for a new place for the Nether Springs as The Grange was not suited to a growing community. Linda and I found a farm for sale, not far from The Grange. There was only a small farm house, but loads of buildings suitable for conversion for community use. We loved it; everyone else hated it. We kept looking.

One morning I had a telephone call.

"Good morning, may I speak to John Skinner?"

"Yes, speaking."

"This is Lord Vinson of Roddam, I believe you are looking for a house in North Northumberland?"

"Yes I am, on behalf of our Community Trust"

"Well I believe I might have what you are looking for. Would you like to see it?"

{pause}

I thought this was one of my mates Dave Hay having a joke.

"Look Dave, you got me. It's over."

"Excuse me?" "What day and time shall we meet?"

We arranged the day and time. Linda and I, plus the Nether Springs trustees and Northumbria Ministries folk trundled over to Hetton Hall. We were met by Lord Vinson and his land agent Peter Guy. Hetton Hall was a 16C fortified pele tower with some Georgian additions, including a derelict stable block. It was in bad shape and needed a refurbishment of the Hall and a renovation of the stable block. Linda and I hated it; everybody else loved it. Lord Vinson proposed a £12,000 a year rent, initially for a three-year period. We would have to put down a £5,000 deposit, the day we signed. If we defaulted on the rent at any time during the three years, we would be liable for a payment of £36,000, minus the deposit. We agreed to discuss the terms and to get back to him. The new trustees were a mix of people from Northumbria Ministries and the Nether Springs Trust. They decided to turn down Lord Vinson's offer. They loved the house, felt the terms were fair, but no one wanted to be liable for £31,000. I rang Lord Vinson to let him know the outcome. He said he had no intention of making the contract with the trustees. He wanted me personally to sign the contract. I explained that I had no money. That didn't deter him. Whatever my circumstances, he said he knew I could make it work. I renegotiated the £31,000 liability. The day I signed the contract and handed him the £5000 cheque, I advised him to hold onto it a few days until there was money in the account. Adrian Beaney promised to gift the money after the sad loss of his father who left him a legacy. This was a shaky start. I knew I needed to put some checks and balances in to support this fledging new trust.

The formation of the Northumbria Community

After 14 years in the making, the Community that no one planned or expected was now emerging and we needed to give it a name: The Northumbria Community. To launch the Community, we organised a series of lectures at Old Bewick church called *Internal Emigres*. It was winter time, people brought blankets and flasks. I gave the first public lectures on Bonhoeffer's new type of monasticism. We now had a new monastic community with a home at Hetton Hall and a new set of trustees and leaders, as in myself, Andy Raine and Roy Searle. However, we did not have an infrastructure or an understanding of how we would maintain our ethos as the Community began to grow. My next task was to present a blue print of what that infrastructure might look like.

The first thing to tackle was the relationship between the trustees and the leaders. As the trustees have certain legal responsibilities (especially regarding financial matters), they often assume the principle decision making role with the leaders implementing their decisions. I made it clear that exercising leadership and taking responsibility could only happen if those making the decisions were also prepared to accept the risks and liabilities. No liabilities meant no responsibility. The trustees had demonstrated when they refused to shoulder the responsibility for the rent at Hetton Hall that they did not want to exercise responsibility when faced with liabilities. This had nearly lost us Hetton Hall. It was agreed: only those willing to shoulder the risks and liabilities would lead the Community going forward. That task would fall to Roy, Andy and I. The trustees would advise, consult and challenge decisions. They could veto any decision that contravened charitable law and procedures because that was their legal responsibility, to exercise what the Charity Commissioners call "due diligence." This decision enabled us to direct the rapid growth we experienced because of the ability to act carefully but quickly.

Next, in the European Church, the Bishops (male) had authority over the clergy and the monasteries. It was a very formal arrangement that reflected their institutional and centralised culture. In the Irish/ Celtic church the Abbots (male or female) looked after the monastic communities, the bishops and clergy, more like a mother or father in a family than a figure of authority. Metaphorically speaking, I became the first "Abbot" of the Community and Roy and Andy "Bishops" (I had a toy car, which had Kermit the Frog and Grouch sitting in the front, with Big Bird on the back seat. When we were tempted to take ourselves too seriously, it was a reminder that I was Grouch, Roy, Kermit and Andy, Big Bird. Nothing more, nothing less).

The idea of mission in the Irish/Celtic Church was tricky. The contemporary Apostles of the Megalomaniac have tried to hold up the Irish as their model - a missional community reaching out to get people "saved." This is not true, thank g-d. The symbols of Irish/Celtic monasticism were the hut and the coracle. When they went out in the coracle, they were exporting a way of life. They were inviting communities and individuals to participate in a new kind of humanity that Christ had won. Everything, everyone was now reconciled to g-d. You were in unless you wanted to count yourself out. Because of unconditional love, it was difficult to escape. G-d was found in the moment now, in the people and places you encountered. Andy had a completely unconscious and simple way of including everyone into the mix.

Roy had been an Apostle of Megalomania, albeit in a diminished form and with a more smiley face. Yet the three master signifiers were operating: you are saved or lost; part of the holy nation or the worldly/evil empire; and a Bible believing Christian. I suggested that Roy drop his itinerant ministry for a minimum of twelve months. He needed to experience his new message - how then shall we live? - which was an enigmatic question rather than a divine solution.

It was at this stage that I started using the metaphors 'monastery' and 'mission' in a new way. Monastery represents the unconditional, the essential failure, waste of time that monasticism is. It has no mission, no intention, no purpose, no teachers, no timescales. It is in this milieu that unconditional love is at home. Mission must come out of the ethos of the monastery. It must reflect its impotence, vulnerability and availability to the (o)ther. The temptations Roy had to overcome were: to not promise things that unconditional love would never deliver, nor try and make the monastic respectable and successful.

Finally, we needed a back of house team, those anonymous people who are the pillars that hold everything up. Sandra and Chris had weathered the storms with us and kept their nerve when it looked like the ship was sinking. We made Sandra the administrator and financial controller of the Community; she was as solid as a rock. Chris Haggerstone agreed to supervise the renovation of the stable block and turn it into a five-bedroom house for our family. Chris is an extremely gifted bloke. In his early twenties he designed, drew the plan and organised the building of his mother-in-law's house. The first job renovating the stable block was to dig out the eighteen inches of chicken poo that covered the whole of the bottom floor. The first day he was bitten by a tick. He was rushed to hospital and overnight deteriorated rapidly with fears that he might get worse. Next day, I phoned Syd Niven, a local pastor. We went to see Chris who was very poorly. Syd prayed for him. I said we couldn't do without him and expected to see him back on site the following morning. Chris turned up the next day and resumed work. Loads of volunteers helped with the renovation: Fred with the carpentry, Gary with the heating; Paul with the painting; and Chris with the electrics.

When money got tight, I would wander the grounds wondering what to do next. It got bad and work stopped. I reminded unconditional love that we were in this mess together, then there was a moment: "I am poor but I will go to the Father for you." Moira came a few days later. She handed me a cheque for £10,000. Work started again. We asked Kev and Ellen Grimley from the Vine Community in Leicester to come to run the house and look after visitors. They were down-to-earth, no-nonsense folk. For those climbing to the top of the tree, Kevin would be regarded as someone who "hadn't made it." Truth is he was one of the wisest people I have met. He was a man of few words but when he did speak, you wanted to listen. Ellen was a curvy, cuddly, part-Italian Mama. She was everyone's Mama, fiercely protective of vulnerable people. This was her strength and weakness. Brenda Grace joined us from Newton Aycliffe. This was the home team.

After his year out, Roy began to build the away teams. We had some great musicians who would form teams and join Roy on the road, sharing what he had learned from the ethos of the Community. The missional side of the Community grew rapidly under Roy's leadership. He would direct people back to Hetton Hall who wanted to explore becoming part of the Community. We held a series of community weekends to give people the opportunity to hang out. Kevin and Ellen mostly led those weekends. Growth was rapid.

During the early days at Hetton Hall, we had a surprise letter from the Bishop of Newcastle Alec Graham. He asked if he could come and visit us. He arrived with his faithful black Labrador and explained he had come to apologise for the way we had been treated by the Church of England. He wanted to invite me to return to the priesthood. The Diocese of Newcastle would pay all the legal fees and he, as my Bishop, would petition the Archbishop of York to restore my orders. That would be interesting. I reminded him that John Habgood, my former Bishop of Durham, was now the Archbishop of York. Having forced me out of the Church why would he want me to return? Bishop Alec seemed prepared for my response. He reassured me that if I agreed to the petition, it would be granted by Archbishop Habgood. Crazy? Linda and I said we would wait a few days and think it over. It seemed the right thing to do for ourselves and the Community. One year later, I was Rev John T. Skinner once again.

The beginning of Community trading

As the Community grew, so did the expenditure required to sustain everything. Hetton Hall became our retreat and study centre. This provided formation to the growing Community and much needed income for the Hall. Mission also provided income as Roy and the teams were paid by the churches and communities they worked with. Members of the Community were happy to pay a small sum into the pot each month or when they could afford it. Others made one-off gifts, small and large. We still struggled to make ends meet. I had to phone the bank manager once a month or more frequently if the overdraft was on the rise to reassure him all was well. Tony Collins, a lad Roy and I were at college with, wanted to sell us his confectionary business. He sold a type of millionaire's shortbread. He was a one-man band and felt the business needed more hands to take it forward. I had spent a year at the University of Durham on a course for potential businesses with a projected turnover of £500K. Without that course, I would never have been able to manage what I was now facing across the different activities of the Community. A couple of us who were experienced in business looked over Tony's figures. They looked promising so we bought him out. Sandra agreed to help set up the new company, rented a small factory unit and hired some folk from the local community to make St. Cuthbert Cake. I helped get the production going.

A few months into production, we encountered two serious unanticipated problems. The first was to do with the customer base: Tony had decided to retain more than 30% of his customers who were near his home. This meant a significant reduction in the turnover we expected. Second, the packaging was not suited to the product. We had to experiment with lots of other products before we got it right. It was tough but business is hard and we started to break even. I liked the idea of a secular work base. It kept us rooted in the local community.

The publication of the Office books

We first published The Northumbrian Office in a leather filo-fax. This was so we could add and subtract as we went along. Andy and I had argued for many days which of the prayers and readings would make it into this edition. He wanted more, I wanted less. He denies this, but look at the two-volume version of the current office book, edited by Andy. I rest my case. We agreed we wanted those prayers and readings that had inspired and influenced us the most on this fourteen-year journey to Hetton Hall. The filo-fax version sold well. Harper Collins picked up the book; they wanted to publish it as *Celtic Daily Prayer* (1994). I was against it, Andy was for it. He agreed to work with them on the editing. It was published in mine and Andy's names and we owned the copyright. The cheques came to me and I signed the money over for Community use. *Celtic Night Prayer* (1996) was next. We asked other members of the Community to contribute a liturgy, reading or prayers for a book that supplemented our original offering. Andy and I edited the book and wrote some of the content. Roy wanted the book to be published "by members of the Northumbria Community." From then on, whatever work Andy and I did, the Community put its name to it. The publication of the Office books created a wave of interest in new monasticism and the Northumbria Community. More growth meant more work.

An emerging vision for European mission

Just before we left The Grange to move to Hetton Hall, I had an experience that would have a profound effect on the direction I thought life was going in. I was sitting in the caravan we had parked on the drive, reading a book Trevor had given me as a present. It was about the history of Irish/Celtic monasticism and its origins in the ministry of St. John the Apostle in Asia Minor. In the book, there was a map of Europe that was full of Irish/Celtic monastic sites. Even though we were just moving to Hetton Hall, I instinctively knew that Europe was to be next on our journey. Our friends Ant and Clare Grimley started taking an interest in Ireland. Roy also began to see Ireland as another important place in our story. In the days and years ahead, we would witness the emergence of the Celtic Arc, a movement of people from Turkey to Ireland and Ireland to Turkey. We began to study The House That John Built, the memories, language and traditions that link Turkey with Irish/Celtic monasticism and the important links across Europe.

Well, I don't know about you but I am exhausted. Those were great years, challenging at times and somewhat disruptive, but the moments of synchronicity between unconditional love and this vulnerable emerging community were just great to participate in! Great memories, great times!

I had nearly finished my work in Northumbria. I just needed to complete these final two years and get the Community Council in place, leaders prepared and a solid infrastructure put in place to support the coming growth. I had no idea that at the end of my two years and the delivery of what I had promised, Linda, our children and I would end up penniless and homeless when the Community did not follow through with their side of the agreement. I really need your help now to ask the question: what was the purpose of distance, diminish, delete?

5. REDEEMING THE PAST

It was the philosopher Walter Benjamin (1892-1940) in his work *Thesis on the Philosophy of History* (1940) who described what he calls "the common-sense view of history." From the common-sense standpoint, history travels in straight lines in a continuous series of events or episodes that can be accounted for in a narrative/story. For Benjamin, the common-sense view of history corresponds to the gaze of those who have won or, to simplify, history is written by those who have won a traumatic struggle. This could be on the international stage such as the French Revolution or a more domestic event such as a bitter betrayal or a gross breach of trust. The narrative is then written in a way that deliberately denies what failed so that the embellished story of what *really* happened can establish itself and support those who won. The only way of redeeming the past is to revisit it, isolate the details from the context and bring them into the open. This is what I plan to do in this chapter.

You may remember Joseph and his Coat of Many Colours? A favourite Bible story. The gist of it is as follows: Joseph was the favourite son of Jacob. Rachael, Jacob's second and favourite wife had given him two children in his old age. Jacob made Joseph a coat of many colours as a sign of his love and affection. The coat and the fact Joseph was a bit of a cocky young lad made his half-brothers crazy with jealousy; they hated him. When the opportunity came, they plotted to kill him. They ended up selling him as a slave. Joseph then went through terrible experiences, including being put in jail. It turns out well in the end: he is made second in command to the Egyptian Pharaoh (King) and is reunited with his family who he forgives. His brothers are shamed by their actions before he reconciles with them.

Early in 1997, my friend John Patterson paid us a visit at Hetton Hall. During his stay, he said something rather odd, "They want your coat." I had no idea what he meant. "They want your coat." It turned out that he was referring to the Joseph story. He felt the "brothers" here were planning to get rid of me. No way! Never for one minute would either Roy or Trevor (my brother-in-law) do anything to hurt me or my family. Anyway, everyone knew I was planning to hand over the reins to them and head off to Turkey.

In this chapter, it will become clear (without any manipulation of the story) that the leaders of the Northumbria Community Roy Searle and Trevor Miller and members the Community Council failed to honour the terms of the succession plan agreement and cut all ties with myself and Linda. This had catastrophic results for our family that would continue for many years. I did not see this coming nor was I able to explain at the time why it happened. These were people I trusted and had invested in. I was shocked.

I now want an answer to these questions:

(i) Was our disastrous exit the result of a messy succession plan and a weakness in leadership to make decisions?

(ii) Was it a messy transition that created unexpected opportunities to cut all ties to me, both relationally and financially?

(iii) Was it a pre-planned strategy by one or more individuals within the leadership and Community Council to cut all ties when the moment was right?

I hope you will join me in this task.

Succession planning is a process for identifying new leaders who can replace old leaders when they leave, retire or die. There are lots of books written about it, a sign of what a crucial process it is. We had put a pretty good succession plan in place to ensure a smooth transition of power, as well as the development of a good infrastructure for the Community Council. What we had not planned for were the psychological challenges and energies that we would face during the transition.

Community folk now knew that, in two years, Linda and I were leaving and going to Turkey. As the head of the Community, I was in a unique relationship with most people, representing the symbol of unity and authority (I say that as an uncomfortable fact). As a result, I was often the target of negativity from people who had an issue with someone else. During my years leading the Community, I experienced that transference of negativity in very real ways: I was threatened with violence by members and guests; I was verbally abused; and I was a target of lies and gossip. I was a referee in heated disputes and had to expel people for lying and stealing or for continually taking advantage of another's vulnerability. I made enemies without even trying.

We soon discovered that there were those who were very angry and disappointed that Linda and I were leaving Northumberland. Trevor Miller was one of them. He complained that he felt unprepared for the burdens and responsibilities associated with leadership. He was anxious, depressed and suicidal, and felt I had let him down by leaving to go to Turkey. I reminded him that we all agreed that I should go to Turkey and suggested he take some time out and seek medical help, but he seemed to be able to cope and carry on.

The most negative response came from a totally unexpected source: Norma Wise. Norma and Ken Wise were our best friends. We had known them and their children since we were in Newton Aycliffe. They had supported us during the breakdown of our relationship with the Church, at Glanton and with the Community at Hetton Hall. "Auntie Norma" was family to our four children.

In 1997, we were due to go to Turkey and meet up with a group from the Community. The idea was to look at The Little Farm Project, a partnership established with John Patterson to build a house in Selçuk, which the Community was supporting. The day before we left for Turkey, I had a call from John Patterson. He wanted to end our partnership at The Little Farm for reasons I will explain to you in the next chapter. It was a shock and something that could not be sorted out overnight. We set out for Turkey. On our arrival, I told the group what had happened with John. Norma was furious and tore a strip off me in front of the rest of the group. The rest of the week was terrible. I was trying to work things out with John Patterson and had the job of communicating what was going on to our Turkish friends. Norma's mood and tone had a big influence on the group and I started to feel hostility from other people. We have some simple rules when we go to Turkey, especially regarding trying to convert the locals to Christianity. Norma broke them all. This was so out of character, I couldn't understand what was going on.

When we returned to the UK, I had a phone call from Brenda Grace. She was concerned that since Norma had returned from Turkey, she had been bad-mouthing me to anyone who would listen. Like me, she thought this was so out of character for Norma, but was worried this could get out of hand, which it did. I went to see Roy and Trevor and explained the situation with Norma. Soon they would be leading the Community and it would be their job to protect me from the fall-out. I asked them to start with Norma, to call her and ask what was going on. They agreed, but never contacted her. Norma asked to see me directly. I said she should speak with Roy and Trevor first.

In January 1998, there was a Northumbria Community gathering held at Bradford Cathedral. This was to mark the end of the transition from my role as Community leader and to pass on the baton to Roy Searle and Trevor Miller. It was a strange time: there was no thank you for the twenty years we as a family had given to the Community; no thank you for the additional two years we had given (putting our move to Turkey on hold) while we put a Community Council and infrastructure in place; no mention of my new role in the Community; no mention of the succession plan; no keepsake; nothing! At the end of the event, I remember standing to one side as the people present queued to congratulate Roy and Trevor. I could count on one hand the number of people who came over to say thank you to Linda and I. What was happening? Why didn't I see it coming?

Norma and Ken didn't come to Bradford. It was obvious they had already won the sympathy vote from a good number of Community members. As leader of the prayer teams, Norma was an influential person in the Community and she was using that influence to continue an attack on me. I asked Roy and Trevor again if they would speak to Norma as things were escalating. They agreed, but once again they never contacted her. Norma was recognised as being the major supporter of the Skinners. It was now clear that there was no longer an effective opposition in place.

Around the same time, another significant event had taken place. Roy had been negotiating with The Bible Society a contract to deliver their new series: *Telling God's Story*. This was a £250,000 project. He was successful and he and I were invited by the chief executive Neil Crosbie to join him and two of his executives to a formal announcement of the award. We were wined and dined at a very nice hotel and the next day the announcement was going to take place. We were sat at the top table with the Bible Society executive. The other tables had middle management from The Bible Society, together with other groups who thought they were coming to an assessment of all the bids and a judgement made by the Bible Society executive as to who had won the contract. It was clear by the seating arrangements that a decision had already been made. It was upsetting for the other groups that all the work they had produced was not going to be seen, let alone assessed by the Bible Society executive.

Before the meeting started, I asked for a private chat with Neil Crosbie. He confirmed my fears: the groups present thought today was assessment day. Some had been working on their bids for months. Even his middle management had not been told what was going on, yet we had been invited by Neil Crosbie to accept the contract. It was a done deal. I was furious. I felt like a conspirator in a plan I never agreed to. I let him know that I thought his business dealings were underhanded to say the least and that if it was up to me, he could keep the contract. Later, Martin Robinson one of the executives present at that meeting came to visit us at Hetton Hall. He asked to speak with me. I will never forget what he said, "John, I really hope this money doesn't hurt you. I apologise now if it does." I thought it a strange thing to say. He was right: £250,000 pounds is a lot of attitude.

Bradford over, Linda and I were looking forward to our move to Turkey. A few weeks passed and we had seen neither Roy nor Trevor. In fact, we hadn't seen anyone at all. Although the stable block is attached to the Hall, there was, at that time, no connecting corridor. To access the stable block and the community office attached to it, you had to come through our back garden. One day, there was a knock on the door. It was Ali Hutchinson, a Community companion from Manchester. We were really pleased to see her but she looked a little bewildered. She had been told by Trevor that Linda and I did not want to see any Community members so she was not allowed to visit. Ali insisted she was going to see us and was willing to be turned away. We had never asked Trevor to stop people coming to see us. Ali said lots of folk had tried and failed to get to see us. People wanted to know what was going on.

I decided to call a meeting between Roy, Trevor and myself. I wanted to know what plans had been put into place for Linda and I to move to Turkey and take up our new role in the Community. Trevor complained that he was still suicidal and anxious and unable to do the simplest of duties. Roy said funds were low so it was difficult to make any plans. I reminded them both that we had an agreement; I had kept my end of the agreement and they needed to keep theirs. They both inferred that nothing had been written in stone. When I asked what this meant, they were evasive, things would be worked out as and when. I was extremely angry.

This was the agreed succession plan:

1. Abbot General

Although we were moving to Turkey, my new role would be to oversee all of our work in Europe from Turkey to Ireland.

2. The Sonset Trust

We had already established The Sonset Trust as our European arm. Roy was made chairman of the trustees. He would create a Council of Bishops to sow the seeds of new houses in Europe. The Abbot General (me) would ensure they maintained our ethos.

3. St John and St Mary's House

Following John Patterson's decision to pull out of the partnership in Turkey, The Sonset Trust went ahead and purchased a new field to build our new monastic centre. We planned to name it after St. John the Apostle who was buried in our town, Selçuk and Mary Mother of Jesus who St. John brought with him to Turkey.

4. Financial Support

Linda and I would continue to receive financial support from the Community in our new role. Together we would raise the funds to build the new centre.

According to Trevor and Roy, this was not written in stone. In fact, everything I have documented above was laid out carefully in a Special Edition of Caim, The Northumbria Community Newsletter published in November 1997.

It was better than stone and it said at the end: **From the leaders, trustees and Community Council of the Northumbria Community** written in bold print to emphasise the importance of the document and that we all agreed to it. There were also drawings of the new monastic centre planned for Turkey. This was our agreement; this was our succession plan. There was nothing flexible about it.

I realised at that meeting that neither Roy, Trevor nor the Community Council were going to honour the agreement they had made with me. I had delivered on my promise, they had balked on theirs. Not one single person from the Community Council, that's the leaders, trustees, company directors and elected council members had the courage to come and tell Linda and I they had broken their promise. It was a poor omen for the future.

Linda and I were now under a silent siege. We did have two visitors: Ervin Dorschler and Dominic de Saules. They said the Community leaders had sent them. They wanted to know when and how much rent we intended to pay for our house now we were no longer leaders of the Community. I threw them out the house. I was now in touch with my primal anger and in a dangerous place. Linda suggested we go and see Brother Roland Walls, my mentor and friend. Br. Roland suggested we go to Turkey for a while. He said a sinister fog had fallen over the Community and we needed to keep our heads down until it lifted.

Up until telling people we were moving to Turkey, our time with the Community had been challenging but rewarding. Going to Turkey was meant to be an extension of our work, a continuation of our twenty years founding and leading the Community. We enjoyed (or thought we did) good relationships with Roy and Trevor. We had absolutely no idea what was going on. This was made worse by the fact that nobody was speaking to us. It was frustrating and upsetting to be treated in such a way. As a family, we were under enormous stress.

We arranged to fly to Turkey taking our youngest children Sadie and Ben with us. Our eldest daughter Jayne was at university and Sara was already in Turkey. Our Turkish friend Erdinç had rented an apartment for us. We were joined by Rose, a community member who had been living at Hetton Hall. Caught up in the tensions and watching what was happening to our family, she left the Community and joined us in Turkey. Linda and I hoped the change in environment would lift our spirits. The truth is, it had the opposite effect: we hit the bottom very quickly.

Before we left for Turkey, I met Roy in the garden at the Hall. He said he had no idea what was going on and he didn't know what to do. I said to him the solution was simple: he needed to honour the agreement that was made between Linda and I and the Community Council. He also needed to protect us from any ongoing negativity and sort out the people who were fuelling it. He promised faithfully that he would do all of that. Instead, I received news from the UK that Roy had attempted to take control of The Sonset Trust and cut its links with Linda and I. Brian Underwood, a Community member from Earl Shilton and a trustee of The Sonset Trust, had resisted the move. Roy had then called another trustees' meeting. At that meeting, all of the money was withdrawn from The Sonset Trust account. The trustees, apart from Brian Underwood, then resigned and cut their links to the trust completely. The Sonset Trust was cast afloat with only Brian in the boat.

Roy's actions had effectively stranded Linda, me, Sadie and Ben in Turkey with no money to live and no money to return home.

I need to pause for a moment and ask you some questions:

How do you think I felt at that moment in time?

If all this stuff were happening to you, how would you feel?

Well, I wanted to return home immediately. I wanted to beat the shit out of Roy. I wanted him to feel the pain of my thirteen-year-old son who was so upset at what was happening, he stayed in bed most days, depressed. I wanted him to feel the fear and anxiety of my girls Sara and Sadie about what the future may hold. I wanted him to feel the confusion of my eldest Jayne about the hostility we were experiencing from some of our dearest friends. I wanted him to know the brokenness and hopelessness my wife Linda was experiencing every day. I wanted him to experience my guilt at not being able to defend my family from people I had placed my trust in. I wanted him to explain why he was doing this to my family. I still want every one of those requirements to be met.

Brian Underwood kindly bought my family tickets back to the UK out of his own pocket. Thank you, Brian; I'm not sure what we would have done without you. I travelled back first and Kevin Grimley and I headed for Hetton Hall. As usual Trevor and Roy kept out of the way. Just as well they did because my mind was filled with images of my emotionally-wrecked family. My first port of call was Lord Vinson. I wanted to see what my status was with the house. Trevor and Roy had already been and convinced him that I needed to sign the house over to them as only they would be able to make the rent as I no longer belonged to the Community. Next, I received a really upsetting letter from Brother Roland, my mentor and friend. Trevor had been to see him and obviously sold him a story to turn him against me. I immediately went to see him. He wept when I arrived. "I dropped you in it, didn't I?" he confessed. To be honest, he had. I was gutted. When I was in Edinburgh, Kevin had gone to speak to Trevor and Roy. When I arrived back at the Hall, he said I must leave. It was a toxic environment and I needed to get Linda and the family out of there as soon as possible. So that was that. I was too exhausted to fight back. For the last year, I had been getting disabling chest pains. My doctor had diagnosed acid reflux, over production of stomach acid due to stress. I discovered later that I had angina and would need lifesaving heart surgery a year after leaving Hetton Hall. I was beaten and broken.

I have tried in these last two chapters to outline the succession plan agreement between myself and the Northumbria Community Council and how it was carried out. The Council included: community leaders, trustees, company directors and elected community members. This succession plan agreement was published and made public in CAIM, The Northumbria Community Newsletter Special Edition in November 1997. I am sorry to labour this. I am doing so to ensure that the emphasis is on an objective agreement rather than subjective, personal relationships. This avoids the deliberate diversion tactic of "there are always two sides to a story."

Let me explain. I wrote several angry letters to Roy and Trevor and the Community Council following the: 1. Broken Agreement 2. Attempted takeover of The Sonset Trust 3. Removal of money from The Sonset Trust account 4. Transfer of copyright and loyalties for *Celtic Daily Prayer* from myself and Andy to the Community, all of which had devastating consequences on me and my family. In one letter, I advised Roy to cross the street if he saw me coming as I could not accept responsibility for my actions if I met him. In another, I threatened legal action for the transfer of the copyright and royalties for *The Celtic Daily Prayer*. These letters are used as a decoy when people ask about what happened. They are never discussed in the context of why they were written. They are presented as "the other side of the story" without reference to the broken agreement.

I have noticed that abuse, whether it is by an individual, an institution or both, employ similar tactics. It is essential to the abuser(s) that the actual nature of the abuse is kept hidden. Abusers will go to any length no matter how low to accomplish that task. One of the main tactics is to question the character of the person who has been abused. I cannot begin to understand or explain the bitterness that was unleashed on me during those last days at Hetton and in the years that followed. One of the areas where I was defamed the most was in relation to money. I was branded a financial liability with the implication that I was no good at managing money. I have a friend Michael who started a community with his wife Anette in Ireland. They bought and refurbished a derelict farm, restoring houses and building a new chapel and a huge hall for the many hard-up young people who stayed at their camps. They set up a charitable trust so they could raise more money for the work. Within months, Michael and Anette were out of a job, out of their home, out on their ear. The farm was turned into a nice retreat centre for middle-class Christians and the hard-up kids were excluded. Michael said this to me, "John, when there is little money, you are the leader and you manage to get through and get things done, people look on you like you are a saint. When the money is in the bank and people are settled and secure, then you are a financial liability." He then took my hands and looked me in the face, "That's the moment they will get rid of you!" And burst out laughing at the irony of it all.

Another tactic is when the abuser becomes the victim: "Look at what you did to me." Not long after leaving Hetton, I had to have open heart surgery. After the operation, I had a life-threatening infection in the wound. They had to operate again and leave an eight-inch by one-inch open wound in my chest. I had caught a hospital infection, which was thought to be the dangerous MRSA bacteria. I was very ill. My complexion was a pale yellow. My face was gaunt and my gums were receding giving me a skeletal look. My doctor informed me my chances of survival were slim. That same day, I had a visitor from the Northumbria Community Council. My visitor never asked how I was. She spent the whole visit telling me off for treating everyone so badly and leaving them in so much turmoil. This was the posture adopted by the Community Council: "Look at what you did to us."

My favourite story, distributed by Roy, was the Bible story about Saul and David. Saul was an ancient King who was mad with jealousy about one of his commanders David who was more successful than he was. His jealousy and rage and the attempt to hold on to his Kingdom led to his downfall. Now, I don't need to tell you who I was meant to be in that story or Roy for that matter!

I turned to philosopher and historian René Girard and his scapegoat mechanism theory to help me interpret the madness that had gone on around me:

"According to René Girard, owing to human nature, envy gradually builds up in a society until it reaches a tipping point, at which order and reason cede to mob rule, chaos, and violence. To quell this 'madness of the crowds', which poses an existential threat to the society, an exposed or vulnerable person or group is singled out as a sink for all the bad feeling, and the bad feeling bred from the bad feeling" (N. Burton, Psychology Today, 21 Dec 2013).

What René Girard is describing is that age old practice of scapegoating where an animal, an individual or a group of people get everybody else's negativity dumped on them and then they are thrown out of the community. What is worse is that the people doing it get a real sense of well-being and self-righteousness from it. They are saving the community from this wretched person.

Once scapegoating was in place, the process of *distance, diminish, delete* was set in motion.

I asked at the beginning of this chapter:

(i) **Was our disastrous exit the result of a messy succession plan and a weakness in leadership to make decisions?**

(ii) **Was it a messy transition that created unexpected opportunities to cut all ties to me, both relationally and financially?**

(iii) **Was it a pre-planned strategy by one or more individuals within the leadership and Community Council to cut all ties when the moment was right?**

You may feel able to answer those questions now? I would love to hear from you and what conclusions you came to at this junction in the book (my contact details are at the end of the book). If you are unsure, my unexpected encounter with Roy and Trevor I recall in the next chapter will help you make up your mind.

When the removal van pulled away from Hetton Hall, there was not a single person who came to say goodbye. We left as we came, with no money and this time we were homeless too. It takes some hard-hearted and twisted people to do this to your family.

Our real nightmare was about to begin.

Kevin and Ellen Grimley had been so concerned about the hostile environment we had been living in that they made all the arrangements for us to move. The Community had cut us off financially and our family support, a kind of supplemental income from supporters, had also been cut. Norma Wise ran our family support for years but had now spoken to everyone to stop paying into the Skinner family pot. Father Terry, the priest at Kev and Ellen's church paid for the removal van. We found out later that Andy Raine had stood at the window and watched us leave.

We moved into Kev and Ellen's three-bedroom house in Barwell, near Leicester. They shared the house with son Ant, his wife Clare and their two young children Mary and Katie. We had Ben and Sadie with us. Sara stayed in Turkey because there was no room to stay in the UK. Jayne stayed at uni and during the holidays stayed with her boyfriend's parents. There was also Kev and Ellen's dog Rufus and our two Labradors. It was obvious from day one that we wouldn't be able to stay very long. We will be forever in Kevin and Ellen's debt for taking us in, it was a massive thing to do. They of course were cut off from the Community and blacklisted.

We soon moved to Linda's mum's house in Sale, Cheshire. By this time, the stress was getting to us all, especially Ben and Sadie. Their schooling had been disrupted and thank g-d this was now the summer holidays. Linda and I spent hours walking the canal paths with the dogs trying to work out what to do next. We were at rock bottom.

My eldest daughter Jayne brought the motivation we needed. She suggested we move back up north and encouraged me to start looking for houses. Syd Niven, our friend and advocate with the Community leaders had been berating them for weeks for cutting us off without any money. They eventually agreed to pay us £500 a month, for six months. It came with a price: I was required to sign over the lease of the house to them. Once again, Brian Underwood came to our aid offering to give us references for any potential landlord and said The Sonset Trust would guarantee the rent. Those positive encouragements gave my severely dinted confidence a boost. We ended up renting a nice family home about fifteen miles from Hetton Hall. Money was tight and I started looking for jobs. Our friends Ali and Alistair gave us a car. We would have been snookered without it.

To check the dates of all these events, I had to read Linda's diaries. Of course, I knew she was suffering but the diaries reveal the true depth of what she was going through, especially the next upheaval. Moving back to Northumberland in 1999 meant we had to get a new family doctor and I went to see him so I could get my insulin and acid reflux medication. Dr Davison was young and sharp. He asked lots of questions about my physical and mental health. After carefully listening, he said I may well have acid reflux, especially with all the stress we had to endure. He also thought I had unstable angina, caused by one or more blocked coronary arteries. Unstable angina can occur at any time and is not induced by physical activity. It is activated mostly by stress. He arranged a stress test that week. You basically run on a treadmill while wires to your chest monitor your heart. After five minutes, the test was stopped. My heart readings were off the chart. I had angina. A few weeks later, I had an angiogram to see the extent of the furring in my arteries. I was in a bad way and needed a quadruple coronary artery bypass urgently. Sara had returned home to the UK and, like me, was suffering emotionally from the trauma with the Community. Dr Davison arranged counselling with a psychotherapist. It was a great help to both of us. Watching the shock and horror in the therapist's face as I recounted the story was reassuring for me. I hadn't imagined it after all.

One heart attack followed the next. I got into the routine of ringing the ambulance, getting admitted to intensive care and returning home a few days later. I was on a long waiting list and knew I couldn't go on like this. Linda was beside herself. She had no support, no one to talk to and little money to keep the home going. After the fifth hospital admission, they agreed to do the operation if I agreed a locum doctor could do it and not my specialist. The operation went well. After four days, I was home. On the second day home, I felt ill. I was rushed into hospital with a serious life-threatening wound infection. I needed another operation. Before I went into the operating theatre, I asked to see the anaesthetist. I asked him to keep fighting for me if anything went wrong that day because I would be still fighting.

During the operation, they had to cut out a long strip of flesh out of my chest to remove the infected area. You would be able to see the chest bone for several weeks until the skin closed naturally. The anaesthetic had affected my throat and during the operation I stopped breathing. They could not get me breathing again. The surgeon was going to call it a day, that would be the curtains for me. Dead. The anaesthetist remembered our conversation and asked to have one more try. He told me he literally stuffed a tube down my throat, creating a passage for me to breath. I woke up in a single room in intensive care. I had two young female nurses looking after me. They were both gorgeous. Still groggy and disorientated I was thinking, "How did I end up here with these two beauties?" "Oh dear! Did I betray Linda?" I knew I could never do that. Relieved, I went back to sleep. In a couple of weeks, I would be home.

In the meantime, Linda had no idea what was going to happen. Our families had taken sides with Freda and Trevor so all contact and support had stopped. Still struggling to make ends meet, she wondered every day if she would have enough petrol to drive the one-hour journey to see me. She cried herself to sleep at night. John Winter, my friend from Bible College days heard I was ill. He sent Linda £500 to help. It was a lifesaver.

I insisted on doing my own daily wound cleaning. In hospital, the doctor would come every day, pour iodine straight into the wound and I would pass out with the pain. When the ward sister returned from leave, she went ballistic with the doctor saying he was barbaric. She used a soothing silicone gel and taught me to do it myself to avoid infection. I had three visitors in hospital. I found out later that people who rang the Community to check on me were told I was fine, nothing to worry about and that I didn't want visitors.

Once home, Andy Raine visited. Linda wouldn't let him in the house. She said this was the third time he had either stood by or sided with those who had hurt me and it wasn't going to happen again. A surprise visitor was Neil Crosbie, the Bible Society chief executive. Linda made him wait at the door while she asked me if I wanted to see him. She was angry and upset when I said yes. He said he had heard about my illness and wanted to check on how I was getting on. He said that he was sorry that I had left the Community and that if any work popped up at The Bible Society, he would give me a call. As he got up to go, he looked nervous and paused for a moment, "Are you planning to write a book?" he asked. "What kind of book?" I replied. "Oh, you know, a kind of autobiography or something like that?" he smiled sheepishly. Linda was right. "Don't let the bugger in, he's after something." I found out later that Neil Crosbie had just survived one outrage, he was hoping I wouldn't cause another.

After a few weeks recovering, I managed to find a job as the manager of a care home for senior citizens. I absolutely loved it! It was a first step away from letting my life be defined by other people. The home was part of a privately-owned group of three residential centres. It had twenty-three beds but only eleven were occupied, a recipe for financial disaster! The owners were desperate for me to turn it around. There was an area manager, Victoria, a young woman who was business savvy. I could see she had her hands full with the money-motivated owners. I agreed to take the job for a considerable salary rise and the freedom to do it my way. With Victoria's support, I could turn this around. The owners had a custom of coming every Monday morning to check if any beds had been filled. It was a pressure my staff and I could do without, so I put a stop to it and said I would report to them on the phone. After two weeks, I realised the problem with getting clients to stay at the centre was because the standard of care was rubbish. There was a culture of disrespect and in some cases, abuse of clients. There was a bad apple on the staff. She came from a trouble-making family and set the tone among the staff for patient care. Following the due procedures, I sacked her and two other members of staff. Her son came to the centre to sort me out but left abruptly after I had a quiet word with him in the car park. I then employed some new staff, started a training programme and began changing the culture of disrespect and abuse to one of respect and care.

Many residential care homes are often set out and run like a death-waiting room. Apart from the TV, there is very little emotional and social stimulation. I appointed an activities officer with a brief to create an individual social diary for all the residents and daily group activities. Each carer was required to get the life story of each person in their care with as many photographs and illustrations as possible. Soon the place was buzzing. I then contacted the social workers who placed residents in care centres, they loved the changes. They also informed me that they needed special places for residents with EMI (Elderly Mentally Impaired) requirements, for example dementia. With the social workers' help, we upgraded to EMI status. Within three months, the centre was full, with a healthy waiting list.

I loved this job and received more from the residents than I gave. My best memory of this time was a resident called Mary. Her son had called at the centre to ask if I would consider taking his mum as a resident. According to her present care plan, she had mini strokes that had resulted in challenging behaviour and aggression. Her son lived in the USA and was worried she was not getting the care she needed. I agreed to go and see her. Walking into her care home, the first thing that struck me was the smell of urine, covered over with a sweet and sickly air spray, always the first sign of neglect. Mary was sitting in the corner of a dark and dingy room. She was rocking back and forwards. Her eyes were glazed over suggesting she was being chemically-coshed (over-medicated to control mood). I decided there and then that I needed to get her out of there. I did a deal with the manager to dispense with some of the formalities related to discharge. She was showered and changed, bag packed and in my car on the way to her new home. Looking at her care plan, my suspicions were confirmed: she was being chemically coshed. I had the doctor prescribe a gradual weaning off the drugs used to sedate her. It took nearly a week. Mary turned out to be a real sweetie. She had memory difficulties but not challenging behavioural problems. I spent many days with her looking over her precious photo albums. She was an elegant lady, a head teacher who had lived a full life. When her son came from the USA to visit her, she looked up at him and smiled, "Hello my darling boy, how nice to see you." A magical moment.

It was discovered that the owners of the group had been skimming money off the company for years. Liquidation loomed. I was angry but thankfully my home would survive and our residents would not be uprooted. I had enjoyed my year there. It had been a healing and uplifting experience. I hoped that Linda and I might now set off for Turkey.

Linda had other ideas. She kept repeating that we needed to go West before we go East. I started to look for church jobs and eventually was offered two potential places in Wales by Archbishop Rowan Williams. While job searching, I came across an advert for an assistant priest in the Parish of Pembroke in Bermuda. I had no idea where on earth Bermuda was located, I was only familiar with the jokes about the Bermuda Triangle.

I discovered it was a tiny number of dots just off the east coast of the USA, a collection of islands joined together, twenty-one miles long and one-mile wide. With nothing to lose, I applied for the job. Much to my surprise, Fr. Gary the priest in charge of the parish rang me up. I was invited for an interview and Linda was to accompany me.

Bermuda was once the playground of the rich and powerful from the USA. Its turquoise sea and pink beaches are more beautiful than you can imagine. It is a leading financial centre and offshore tax haven and a leading player in the financial and insurance sector. It also has a history of slavery, civil war, political unrest and the assassination of a British Governor (Bermuda has been a British Overseas Territory since 1707). Racial tensions still dictate the political climate in Bermuda today.

At the interview for the job, I was asked by a black Bermudian if I was racist. I thought for a minute and replied, "Yes. I am British. Racism is in my DNA. Do I condone racism? No, I would oppose it in myself and publicly." Although the interview went reasonably well, I wasn't confident I had done enough. My history with the Church of England didn't help. At the airport, we were waiting for departure when a message came over the loud speaker, "Would Fr. John Skinner please report to reception? Thank you." At reception, I was handed a telephone. It was Fr. Gary. The selection committee wanted to offer me the job as assistant priest. I accepted. We were Bermuda bound.

We spent two and a half years healing in Bermuda, from 2001 to 2004. Pembroke Parish had three churches: St. John's, once the white colonial church; St Monica's mission church, built by black Bermudians; and St Augustine's mission church built by West Indians. My brief, after consultation with government representatives, business leaders and the local community, was to initiate an urban renewal plan around the two mission churches. Both were centres for distributing drugs. My first job was to earn the trust of the drug dealers. St Monica's was in the most deprived area in the city. We decided to commit to an urban renewal programme around St Monica's. This would include: (1) a state-of-the-art computer suite in the unused basement of the church. Daytime it would be used for kids expelled from school and evenings for kids without computers or internet access. There would also be a neighbourhood office for support and advice; (2) a piece of derelict land near St. Monica's church would become a memorial park, named after one of its community activists. Young families would have a safe and much needed play area and older folk a place to relax; and (3) an outdoor sports complex for basketball, cycling, athletics, baseball, music concerts, public gatherings, with a children's play area built in, right in the heart of the community.

I organised a community trust so we could raise money directly and decide how to spend it. I met with local businessmen, including a former Prime Minister, to solicit support for each stage of the work. They were brilliant, sharing their experiences and giving funding. The first new black national government offered funding and practical support such as plant and machinery. It was a real community effort and the project began to be realised. At St. Augustine's, we refurbished the church and the hall and conscripted members from St John's to support the ageing congregations.

In Bermuda, Linda and I regained our strength to lift our heads again. I received a commendation from the Prime Minister's Office for my work and the promise of an extension to my work permit if I wanted to stay for another term. Job done, we were ready to return to Turkey.

As we began to look at our Turkish options, I had an email from John Patterson. You will remember we were in a partnership to build a centre in Selçuk (Ephesus), Turkey. He apologised for dissolving our partnership and asked if we could start again. I was going to need some convincing. He kept up the emails and pleaded with me to renew our friendship. Eventually I agreed to go and look at where The Little Farm Project was up to. This was in February 2004. The utilities John and I had installed such as a well, electric pylons and gas tank were still in place. A new stone and steel fence now surrounded the property. The house I designed was now complete, although it was an empty concrete shell and would need fitted out completely. The garden would need landscaped including new walls, steps, paths, trees and a drive. We also needed another building to act as an office. I agreed to complete the house with our Turkish friends Erdinç and Kemal who had built it. John transferred the remaining money he had raised to our Turkish account. I then took on the financial responsibility to complete the house and the additional works. Erdinç agreed to complete the fitting out of the house by the 29th May 2004. Linda and I would arrive then with a group of Bermudians who we were going to lead a two-week holiday tour. It was "Goodbye for now Bermuda" and finally, "Hello Turkey, our new home."

6. THE HOUSE THAT JOHN BUILT

In the summer of 1992, Linda and I were packing boxes at The Grange, ready for our move to Hetton Hall. I was feeling depressed and decided to spend a day reading in the caravan that was parked on our drive. Trevor had bought me a book on the history of the Irish/Celtic Church and I thought I would look over it. It is difficult to concentrate when you are depressed so I gave up reading and just looked at the illustrations in the book. One of them was an old map that showed the movement of early Christianity from Asia Minor across Europe to Ireland. Then I had what I would describe as an "unwelcome" moment: "This is next dear one, this is next." "I hope not!" were my first thoughts. We had Hetton Hall ahead first before any European odyssey, thank you very much.

The next day, I had a phone call from John Patterson. It was an invitation to travel to Turkey with him to a conference. He then wanted to take me to a place called Selçuk because he had an intuition we needed to spend some time there. "No, thank you!" was my response. There was no way I wanted to go to Turkey. A few days later, John Patterson rang again. He repeated the invitation and said I should think it over. "No, thank you!" I had Hetton Hall looming and could not spare the time to go to Turkey.

A few days later, I went to bed early and had an odd dream. A man came into my bedroom and tapped me on the shoulder. I woke up startled but he said not to worry, I could go to sleep again in a moment. He said I should be prepared to travel to Turkey as a tourist, nothing else. A few days later, John Patterson rang again and suggested I come to Turkey as a tourist. He also gave me an update on the history of Selçuk. I was amazed to discover modern Turkey was in Asia Minor. I was going as a tourist to a place on the old map I had just been looking at! I agreed to go and suggested he start making the arrangements.

In the meantime, we were off to Hetton Hall. We moved in in October 1992. It was freezing cold. At night, I would sit with my feet in the warming shelf of the oil heated Aga with my jumper pulled up over my face and head, smoking my pipe through a hole in the wool. We had to live in the main Hall while we raised the money to renovate the old stable block, which would become our family home. The kids absolutely hated it, sharing the space, especially the bathrooms with the growing number of visitors we received. My eldest Jayne could often be heard knocking on a bathroom door demanding to be let in so she could get ready for school.

We translated the life we had been living and learning at The Grange into a community context at Hetton Hall. Linda established a monastic day with a daily rhythm of prayers from the Northumbrian Office, a schedule of work (sharing chores, gardening, restoration work), a period of daily study, "pottering" (an intentional meaningless activity), eating, drinking and sharing stories.

In January 1993, I headed off to Turkey with John Patterson. We arrived at Istanbul airport and took a taxi to one of the suburbs. It was lightly snowing and when we got out of the taxi, the smell of smoke caught the back of my throat and made my eyes water. I felt like I had walked into a Charles Dickens novel in Victorian England with smoky coal fires and a dusting of snow.

We were staying with John Taylor who had come as a missionary to Turkey from London. John shared his ground floor apartment with a lad from America whose name evades me. It was late when we arrived, so after drinking some black Turkish tea, served in small glasses with a lump of sugar, we headed for bed. John Patterson and I were sleeping on the floor in what appeared to be a utility room. It was a disturbed night. The plumbing in the apartment block was a nightmare. Every time someone in the flats above flushed their loo, the contents would end up in the loo in our apartment. I will let you imagine the results. Then there was the rat. One of the ventilation pipes had a hole in it and every now and again a rat would jump out onto a nearby shelf, forage, then jump back in. I was sleeping on an old army style blow-up bed made of heavy-duty rubber. As my body heated up, so did the rubber and when I got up the next morning, I smelled like a rubber band which lasted the whole day. This was poor Istanbul and the perfect location for missionaries. Istanbul is as elegant and sophisticated as any European city.

That day, after a little sightseeing, we headed off for a Christian conference. This was a gathering of missionaries with their groups of Turkish converts or expats looking to connect with other like-minded people. This was an Americanised group that had come to Turkey "to fly the flag of freedom" and "take Turkey for Jesus" (that was the theme of the conference). I noted that the Turks present were from the poorer and uneducated classes; several looked malnourished and others were presenting symptoms of mental health issues. Joining up with the Megalomaniac in that era in Turkey would almost certainly mean being turned out of your family and loss of your job if you had one. A high price to pay for commitment to a dangerous and deceitful ideology. It seemed to me that these folks needed their lives upgraded and improved in this life rather than wait for the life to come.

After Istanbul, John Patterson and I headed down to Selçuk. Although it is only a small town (population approx. 32,000), it is one of the most visited tourist attractions in modern Turkey. Selçuk is only one mile from the ancient Greek city of Ephesus, built in 10BC. For centuries, it was home to Greek, Roman and Byzantine civilizations before it suffered several earthquakes and the harbour, the source of its prosperity, silted up. The Temple of Artemis, one of the seven wonders of the world, was in Ephesus. However, only the foundations and a few artefacts are left. The rest of the Temple was pilfered to build the Basilica of St John and the Isabey Mosque.

Ephesus was part of Asia Minor and, outside of Israel, was the single most important region for Christianity. Several biblical characters visited or lived here. The most famous were Mary Mother of Jesus and St. John the Apostle, the disciple Jesus loved most. The Emperor Justinian built a Basilica in memory of St. John and to house his remains. Mother Mary travelled to Asia Minor with St John after the death of Jesus. She lived in a house on nearby Nightingale Hill, no doubt for her safety. It is a treasured centre of pilgrimage and tourism. St. Paul, the famous apostle of Christianity, started a church in Ephesus and it spread throughout Europe (Forgive the history lesson. I have only included it, especially the information about the region's importance to Christianity, because it features in this chapter).

John Patterson had visited Selçuk before and stayed at a "pension" (a bed and breakfast) belonging to a retired school teacher Kemal. It was a very simple affair. Kemal had a two-storey house with various outbuildings he had converted into bedrooms. Its best feature was the courtyard garden where we would eat a very simple Turkish breakfast of boiled eggs, cucumber, olives, tomatoes and freshly baked bread. We would sit in the shade of the lemon tree, surrounded by old olive oil tins filled with plants and flowers.

John Patterson did treat me like a tourist. We visited the Basilica of St. John, Ephesus and Mother Mary's House. On an evening, we would go into the small town and eat egg and chips at Çetin's restaurant and watch football or any sport we could find on the TV. John knew quite a lot of missionaries and there was a tension and suspicion between the Turks and the missionary community. He advised me never to trust a Turk. I said I could never do that and I planned to treat Turks the same as everyone else (it is ironic that the only Turk who has ever hurt me is a convert to Christianity).

It was right to come to Selçuk as a tourist. There was a lot to take in, people to meet and new cultural perspectives to learn and respect. John was also right about his intuition that something special was happening here. I was in Asia Minor. I had visited the Basilica of St. John, regarded as the Father of Irish/Celtic Christianity. This was the birthplace of The House that John Built, but it was time to return to Northumbria and unpack my thoughts and responses to Turkey.

Things were gathering pace in Northumbria as more and more guests found their way to Hetton Hall. The challenge was to offer hospitality, in a consistent and caring way, to individuals and groups from different social and religious backgrounds. Br. Roland had taught me that a community has neither the time, experience nor resources to offer hospitality to everyone. Who should, and better still, who could we welcome? Most people who found their way to us, did so because they were experiencing a similar kind of crisis that we had first encountered many moons ago. They were losing confidence and certainty in their religious beliefs and practices. It was a relief when they discovered other people were in the same boat. They wanted to know how we were coping with this seemingly unexpected crisis, what was causing it, and how it would all end up. In response, we started Northumbria Community weekends when, from Friday evening through to Sunday afternoon, people could come and we would go through the basics of the Community Rule and let them experience the monastic day. We also ran retreats through the week where we could share the sources which we had found helpful, like the Desert Mothers and Fathers and the early Irish/Celtic communities. We used to close the house in January to rest and recover and explore some of the philosophical themes that had fuelled the crisis of confidence in religious experience. That job fell mostly to me, and I enjoyed watching people connect with the source and cause of some of their experiences and, in doing so, remove the fear and uncertainty they caused.

We also decided to take one or two people at a time whose life circumstances or mental health issues meant they needed support and refuge for a time. One person was recommended by a local pastor as having depression and anxiety. I discovered that he had a long-term acute psychiatric condition that required medication to keep his condition under control. He got more and more paranoid and was convinced I was plotting to kidnap or kill him. As a result, he attacked me one night with the poker we used for the coal fire. He had to be restrained and taken to hospital. This was a lesson learned about only being able to offer hospitality to those you should and could care for. We built long and lasting friendships with the many people we supported.

The biggest challenge was making sure the kids, both our own and other people's, were kept safe. We had three girls and one boy all under thirteen when we first moved to Hetton Hall. People who have a sexual interest in children tend to hang out around communities. We already had experience of this around Easter workshop when I had to expel a man who was grooming one of the community teenagers and report him to the police. A lot of mums and dads see community gatherings as a form of communal babysitting. We had to encourage the more laid-back parents to be a little bit more vigilant around their kids and to not leave them alone with adults they did not know and clearly trusted.

During my time at The Grange, I was asked to help a sex offender. Before I agreed, Chris, Sandra, Linda and I sat down to discuss the implications of it all. We agreed that I should do it, providing he accepted zero tolerance rules regarding boundaries in relationship to our kids. He was never, under any circumstances, to be left alone with them. Social Services turned up one day with a police officer. They complained that I was putting my children at risk by helping this man and was at risk of having them taken into care. I explained my relationship to this person and the boundaries we had placed around our children. The police officer went to confirm my comments with Chris and Sandra who said the same thing. I could continue to see him.

Back at Hetton Hall I decided to read the book Trevor had bought me. It was a fascinating read. It told the story of the spread of Christianity via the community of St. John in Asia Minor across Europe to Ireland and back again. As one of the people losing faith in European Christianity, finding out about the faith and life of these early Irish-Celtic communities was much more than an academic exercise, it was an exercise in hope.

At the beginning of 1993, we organised an open day to introduce the wider community to Hetton Hall. Ant and Clare Grimley organised a dance-drama presentation called *The Brendan Voyage*. This followed the travels of St. Brendan who set off from Ireland, with 14 other monks, for an adventure in unknown waters, searching for Paradise. This was in the 5th century, when the world's seas and oceans were still unchartered territory. They built a primitive boat out of wattle and animal skin called "a currrach." *The Voyage of St. Brendan* was written in 900AD. It captures the mystery and mythology of the epic odyssey and became a classic in European literature. It is believed that Brendan and his companions reached Greenland and, as a result, discovered North America centuries before Christopher Columbus. This belief was given plausibility when a group of modern adventurers, led by Tim Severin, replicated the circumstances of *The Brendan Voyage*, including a replica of the boat and sailed 4,500 miles from Ireland to Newfoundland. I was very moved by this presentation and sensed that being open to travelling The House That John Built was something we needed to consider, both as a family and as a Community.

That same year, John Patterson and I returned to Selçuk. We stayed at Kemal's pension. It was summertime and the temperatures were in the mid to late thirties. That kind of heat slows your pace and it is challenging just moving around. Bedtime was worse. The bedrooms had no aircon and if you opened the windows the mosquitos would get in and eat you alive. You slept fitfully, in a puddle of your own sweat, longing for morning to come. From May to October there is little, if any rain in this region of Turkey.

Agriculture and tourism are the two industries that fuel the Selçuk economy. The warm weather also brings the missionaries out. Like migrating birds, they return to warmer climates to peddle the ideology of the Megalomaniac. John wanted me to meet a group of them, including a Turkish Pastor. I had absolutely nothing in common with any of them. I felt strongly that they needed to be rescued from an ideology that poisons hearts and minds. I made polite noises, but resolved not to get involved in any way or form in the missionary community. My place was with the Turks.

During this trip, John Patterson and I began to talk about the possibility of building a community house in Selcuk, not a missionary centre, but a centre of new monasticism, committed to the people of Selçuk. We would use the fundamentals learned in Northumbria, at the Nether Springs, drawing from the Irish/Celtic way of living and allow them to emerge in this very different cultural context.

Back at Hetton Hall, I decided to start conceiving a new adventure. The plan was to make a journey from nearby Holy Island, through Scotland on to France and across Europe to Turkey and back again. This was the geography of The House that John Built. The aim was to investigate the memories, language and traditions of St. John's communities. I made a list of everything we would need to get a family of six safely across Europe. The most expensive but most important thing we needed would be transport. I spent months reading motor home magazines until I knew most models inside out. Even the older models weren't cheap so it would take time to find something. I planned the routes by identifying the most important people and places we needed to visit. I then did a budget of all necessary costs from insurance, breakdown cover, fuel, food, household goods to camp fees, entry fees, ferry fees and clothes. Once I had an idea of the costs, I could start trying to work out how to fund it.

At the end of 1993, John Patterson and I returned once again to Selçuk. We followed our usual routine of eating our evening meal of egg and chips at Çetin's cafe in the village square. Çetin used to be a railway engineer and running a cafe and cooking was a challenge for him. He used to wash his salad stuff in the washbasin of the loo so we kept off the salad. At lunch time, he would always serve lentil soup. I asked if we could have tomato for a change. Next day, he served lentil soup with tomato ketchup in it. This visit, Manchester United were playing the Turkish team Galatasaray in the UEFA Champion's League. We ate our egg and chip butties and drank our tea with our eyes glued to Çetin's portable TV. It was an exciting match ending in a 3-3 draw. As soon as the match finished, a crowd gathered in the square opposite our cafe. These were Galatasaray supporters celebrating the epic draw with the famous Man United. Çetin thought that he would let the crowd know we were Man United supporters. A group came over, pulled us out of our seats and into the crowd to join in the celebration. We had to join them chanting Galatasaray followed by Manchester United!

Çetin had a new waiter called Ali. Ali was a small stocky man and had a certain air about him. We discovered that he once was a very successful restaurateur with a string of restaurants. He lost his businesses and his family through gambling and binge drinking. Now in his sixties, he worked as a waiter to keep his head above water. Ali could stay sober for months, then he would go binge drinking for several days. He had been a very generous man during his business years. To the local people, he was a legend and people were happy to offer him jobs and return the kindness he showed them during his better days.

The following evening (the night before John Patterson was due to fly back to the UK), we sat at Çetin's and discussed the possibility of buying some land on which to build a house. Ali must have overheard our conversation and at the end of the evening, he came and sat with us. His shift was over, he had started drinking and was slightly worse for wear. He said if we were serious about buying land, he had a friend who could arrange a plot to view the next day. He said he would meet us at Çetin's at 10am the next day. John Patterson would be on the way to the airport in the morning so it would be down to me to take a look.

I never expected Ali to turn up, but there he was bright and breezy at Çetin's cafe at 10am. The man he had with him was nicknamed "Ali Two Percent," a reference to his status as an estate agent. Two percent was his sales commission. We drove out of town towards a village in the mountains. At the foot of the mountain road, we pulled off onto a dirt road. 400m down the dirt road we stopped at a field that looked like it was used for growing wheat. It was in two parts: a very flat parcel of land with a bank to its rear. I walked up the bank with the field in front. Beyond and to the right of the field were mountains, to the left I could make out the silhouette of the Basilica of St John. "The Little Farm" as we would later call it, had already won my heart.

Ali (the waiter) spoke fluent English so we began to discuss with Ali Two Percent details about the Little Farm and its price. Size wise, it was 7.5 dönüm which is 7,500 m². Current planning (if approved) meant we could build a house 250 m². It was owned by a family and all had agreed to sell. Next, it was down to the price. Ali (the waiter) told me the price in Turkish lira, which at that time was calculated in the millions and billions. I got out my trusty calculator, entered the lira price and divided by the exchange rate into sterling. "How much?!" I heard myself say out loud, "You must be joking!" Ali (the waiter) looked hurt and offended. He took the calculator from me with its £77,700 calculation. He made a few adjustments and handed it back to me. It said £7,770. I was embarrassed. I had got the decimal point in the wrong place. I apologised to everyone and agreed to buy it. A handshake does the deal in Turkey. Ali Two Percent and I shook hands and I became the joint owner, with John Patterson, of a field in Turkey.

I was excited and a little anxious walking back to Kemal's pension. There was one hiccup in the plan: we had no money. However, I had proven many times in the past that if you commit to a plan, it must be a calculated risk. It mustn't be something ridiculous and out of reach but one that can be realised, even if it stretches you to the limit. Back at the pension, Mandy was waiting for the news. She was from John Patterson's church and had travelled there with him. "We have bought a field!" I announced excitedly. We sat and drank Turkish tea, ate biscuits and I told her about the events of the day. As I finished, Mandy said she had more good news. She worked as a house cleaner and recently one of her clients had died. In her will, she had left Mandy £40,000. She was going to give John Patterson and I £10,000 to buy the field and pay all the fees to get started.

John Patterson was excited about the purchase and, a few months later, we returned to Turkey with a briefcase full of money. At the Turkish currency exchange bureau, we spent forever negotiating an exchange rate and finally left with the equivalent of 4 briefcases full of lira. We wanted to get the deal done as soon as possible but had discovered before we returned to Turkey that we could not put The Little Farm into mine or John Patterson's name. Foreigners were not allowed to own property in the countryside at that time. John Patterson suggested we ask the Turkish pastor he had introduced me to on an earlier visit. To be honest, I disliked this man because he reminded me of the "holy men" from my childhood: all appearances and no substance. As a result, they were schooled in deceit and manipulation. The problem was we had no other contacts, other than Kemal. To be honest, I would have felt better putting the house in Kemal's name, but the pastor, on the surface, was the best option, he was "one of us."

We visited him and he laid down his ground rules for signing his name on the "tapu" (deed of ownership):

1. **We must ensure that he does not incur any financial liabilities from this agreement;**

2. **He would not be required to spend any of his own money on the project;**

3. **He would not be required to supervise, visit or have any active role in the building stages;**

4. **We would be required to find a responsible person(s) who could oversee the project to whom he would give his POA (power of attorney) to act on his behalf as the legal owner;**

5. **As soon as the laws changed in our favour, we would pay the fees to have the tapu transferred from his name into ours.**

I wanted to get it all in writing but John Patterson said it would be offensive to make such a request. That was a mistake.

House bought and signed for, we began the task of getting started. Kemal had three daughters, and one of them Nesrin was married to Erdinç. Erdinç was a local business man, well-known and respected for his honesty and integrity. Kemal and Erdinç agreed to build our house. They wanted no money, only the solemn promise it would not be used for missionary purposes. John Patterson struggled with that; I was delighted. No missionaries, yes! We made a solemn promise.

John Patterson and I sat in Çetin's restaurant one evening and I described to him the design for a house that could work for a community living on the site and he drew it on a napkin. We had that napkin drawing translated into an architectural plan and submitted it for the planning application. It would take a couple of months to get a decision. When it came through, permission was declined. There was a dry river bed which filled with mountain water during the winter. When full, it effectively cut the proposed house off from the main road, which was unacceptable to the planners. Linda and I were in Turkey at the time and agreed to see what we could do about it.

We had been invited to dinner by a local politician who was also a strong nationalist. I guess he wanted to check us out. His first question was to ask if we were missionaries. I could honestly say "no" with some vigour. I did tell him I was a priest and that the Anglican Communion had a church in nearby Izmir, used by foreigners for more than three hundred years. He asked my opinion about missionaries. I was careful not to berate any individuals, but said I did not share their ideological beliefs. We had a pleasant evening during which he flirted with Linda throughout. I told him about our failed planning permission. He said not to worry, he would sort it out for us the following day. We discovered later that he was once a senior planning manager. He went into the planning office the next day and simply crossed out the river from our plan. It was later approved. We could start building.

Over the next two years, John and I begged and borrowed to get The Little Farm project moving. Kemal and Erdinç were brilliant and it was their effort that made it all possible. We managed to get two electric pylons in place and drill a well 55m into the ground. It is impossible to do anything well in Turkey without a Turkish family or partner. During this time Kemal and Erdinç became our friends and family.

With the Little Farm project in the safe hands of Erdinç and Kemal, and me now back at Hetton Hall, I decided to finalise the plan for our European adventure. One of the Community members offered to lend me the money to buy a camper van and the Community agreed to fund the journey. I eventually found an old Mercedes camper van. It was originally a 507d delivery van which had been professionally converted. There were 6 beds: a double at the back of the van, two singles in the middle and two children's beds in the overhead roof compartment. We nicknamed it "The Beast" because it was a big, solid and intimidating vehicle. It would take us four months to complete our journey to Turkey via several European countries. We would travel several hours every day, visiting historic sites and locations. On an evening, we would check into a campsite with a pool so the children could relax and let off steam. There was the odd quip at home that the Skinners were on "an extended holiday," far from it.

When we arrived in Spain, temperatures were in the high forties; the heat wave claimed many lives. The tarmac was melting on the roads and you could only go outside for short periods of time. The Beast had no air conditioning and, worse, the heater was broken and the fan was stuck on full, circulating the hot air. I was exhausted with driving. We decided to ask Kevin and Ellen Grimley to join us. We were relieved when they flew into Spain, wearing their straw hats. We took turns sleeping in The Beast or outside in a tent. It was a relief making it to Turkey in one piece. The Beast did us proud.

We repeated the trip in 1997 with the intention of making a video presentation of The House that John Built and to carry out more research. Unfortunately, we had to cut the trip short as Kevin got news of a death in his family. We returned to the UK from Italy (Linda is currently working on an illustrated book documenting those two journeys, which will be available 2018).

It was at the end of the 1997 trip when I got a phone call from John Patterson saying he no longer wanted to work with me. This was on the eve of travelling to Selçuk with a community group to see the progress at The Little Farm. What was the reason for such a drastic change of heart?

Earlier that year, John had asked me to visit his church to see if I could help sort out tensions in the leadership team. The rest of the leadership team thought it wise to invite the official overseers of the church into the mix as they had the authority to address any issues that might turn up. I worked closely with the team. It turned out that John was regarded as the source of the tensions in the leadership. This was something that could be sorted out providing there was a willingness to address it. However, the overseers of the church also uncovered a personal matter that would require John Patterson to step down from the leadership team. This was not my doing and I may have handled the situation differently.

A few weeks later, John Patterson's replacement visited me at Hetton Hall seeking my advice. One of the topics he wanted to discuss was money: John Patterson was still being paid his full salary by the church. The new leader was concerned because they could barely afford it and there was no sign of John Patterson being able to return to his job in the foreseeable future, if at all. He wanted to give a month's notice and stop John Patterson's salary completely after that. My advice was to suggest he went back to Coventry and speak with John Patterson directly and propose a term of notice between 3 and 6 months during which John Patterson would continue to be paid while he looked for other employment. When the new leader returned home, he bottled out. He gave John Patterson a month's notice and then stopped his salary. When asked by John Patterson if I had proposed the salary cut, he let him believe I did. I only found this out many years later, when I was sent an apology. John and Marg Patterson felt I had betrayed them, both with the decision to take John out of leadership and to stop his salary. Neither of these decisions had been mine but no amount of dialogue would convince them otherwise. They effectively ended our long-term relationship.

Once we arrived back in Turkey, I told Kemal and Erdinç about John Patterson's decision. They advised me to stand back from it all and they would help me find another field. In the meantime, they would continue to help John Patterson build the house they had started, in the hope our relationship could be restored in the future.

When I returned to the UK, I took the photographs of a possible new field to show the Community Council. It was agreed that we should try and raise the £17,500 it would cost to purchase it. Jill and Jeff Sutheran wanted to lend the Community the cash to buy the land. I already had an offer from someone for whom it would have been much less of a risk if things went wrong. However, Jeff and Jill insisted that they wanted to take that risk themselves as they firmly believed in the new focus on Europe. The money was loaned to The Sonset Trust. Buying the field would be a major factor in restructuring the mission of the Community around The House That John Built. We would now have a European focus from Turkey to Ireland.

Only months after buying the new land, our relationship with the Community went pear-shaped. All the money was removed from The Sonset Trust and the Sutherans demanded the money they'd loaned the trust be returned to them. When asked by one of our trustees why they wanted to disinvest from something they had insisted on being part of, they blamed me. It was me, they claimed, who had taken their money, a rumour that was circulated within the Community, adding to my notoriety.

I wrote in the last chapter that the next five years were catastrophic for us as a family. There was no time, opportunity or money to develop the field in Turkey. The Sonset Trust had been left in debt and without any supporters. Rumours and innuendo circulated that painted the picture that I had been the cause of the breach in relationship with no reference whatsoever to the agreement that had been broken by Roy and Trevor and the Community Council. The one thing that kept us going was the knowledge that we had to go to Turkey.

During our recovery period in Bermuda from 2001 to 2004, I was surprised that John Patterson contacted me. His apology for breaking our partnership in 1997 and his request for me to start over again was a genuine surprise. For many years, John Patterson had been my role model. My last encounter with him revealed some weaknesses in his character and leadership skills. Had he been able to address them and learn from them? He assured me he had. If Linda and I returned to Turkey alone, we would have support from Kemal and Erdinç. We had few supporters, even less resources to develop the community house. John Patterson was offering a renewal of our partnership. If we joined forces again, we could move the whole thing forward very quickly. I have been told this has been a major weakness in my leadership skills: choosing potential over attitude, expediency over foresight. I knew it was a huge risk to renew my partnership with John Patterson but I decided to take it because it would be the fastest route to get the Little Farm up and running.

After a couple of weeks back in Selçuk, I realised things were not what they seemed. I discovered John Patterson had been helped with the finance towards the development of the Little Farm from a church in America. They had been told that the Little Farm would become a home/orphanage/centre for street children from the nearby city of Izmir and a missionary centre for the Aegean region. They weren't the only ones: a British charity had given a significant sum of money towards resourcing a workshop/training facility to teach kids practical skills (I found this out by accident when one of the charity trustees asked me how the workshop was coming along!) This money had not been spent on the workshop/training facility but on other things.

Kemal and Erdinç had found out about the American involvement and the plans for the house. They were furious. First, it was illegal for foreigners to offer charitable services to people who were the responsibility of the Turkish authorities to deal with. This would bring shame and dishonour. Second, to bring street children to Selçuk would cause a political uproar and cause untold problems for Kemal and Erdinç. Far worse, they wanted to know why we were breaking the solemn promise John and I had made to them that the Little Farm would not be used as a missionary centre, an act that would bring shame on their family as they were identified with us. They were deeply hurt.

It got worse. I got some of the Americans together and discovered they knew nothing about the promise made to Kemal and Erdinç about not having a missionary centre. Apart from their leader, they also had no idea who I was, not a good sign. Neither did they know the laws relating to foreign charities. Their leader came from a "kick-ass" American Christian culture, hard-core megalomania. If they wanted to have a missionary centre, then Kemal and Erdinç couldn't stop them! "They are nobodies!" His words. The rest of the group were more sympathetic to the situation, but I knew I would have big trouble with their Kick-Ass leader.

I apologised to Kemal and Erdinç. It would take time to rebuild their trust. I reassured them that, for my part, a missionary centre and street children orphanage were not on my wish list for the Little Farm and I assured them that it was not going to happen.

Good old John Patterson. He had fixed the game, passed me the ball and had gone home.

7. ERDINÇ SÖZER R.I.P

In 1994, I led a group from the Northumbria Community to Turkey. The hotel rejected the bank draft they had requested and asked for cash. I asked the group if everyone could chip in and I would return their cash in the UK, but most declined. I heard things can get a bit difficult if you don't pay your bill with the police often getting involved. I was a bit anxious and decided to go for a walk to see if I could get any ideas about what I could do. I walked past Erdinç's jewellery shop and he asked me in for a cup of tea. I was still distracted and he obviously took notice. "John, why are you so anxious?" he asked. Being British, I said everything was fine and there was nothing to worry about. "John, you are anxious and when you worry you make yourself ill. Tell me what is wrong." I carried on with, "It's okay, don't worry." Erdinç carried on too, "John, you don't understand, I am your friend. I can't let you get ill, you must tell me what is wrong so I can help you and stop you getting ill."

So, I ended up telling Erdinç about the hotel bill. He smiled, opened the till in his shop and started counting money out. "How much do you need?" he asked. I said I couldn't possibly take money from him. He looked at me and said, "Why do you embarrass me by not taking my money? This is about our friendship. Now, how much do you need?" This was the measure of the man, with the same qualities and values he demonstrated time and time again.

It is impossible to understand our lives in Turkey without realising that they were intertwined with Kemal, Erdinç and their families'. Kemal was the big brother to John Patterson and I, referred to as "the Abi" in Turkish. That meant he was required to look after us, watch our backs and promote our wellbeing. I will give you an example: just after we moved into The Little Farm, our neighbours asked if we could let them have water. We asked Kemal what to do. He checked them out and came back with a firm "no". They were known criminals. They went around town asking our friends to help them change our minds. Then they began to threaten them. One day, a local criminal sent a car to Kemal's to take me to his office. Inside, he gave me tea and chatted about what great friends we were. He said our friendship was important to him and he didn't want anything to happen to me or my family so best give our neighbours water. I said no. Finally, remember Ali, the waiter? He got us the land for The Little Farm. He came to me and said I owed him a favour: he wanted me to give my neighbours water. I went to Kemal and Erdinç. Kemal agreed that I owed Ali a favour and we would now have to give the neighbours water. He got Erdinç to arrange a meeting with them in a local tea house.

Kemal, Erdinç and I arrived first. Our neighbours arrived in a BMW 7 series. They entered the tea shop literally dripping in gold with rings, chains, watches and wrist chains. The three of them each greeted me like a long-lost friend with hugs and the traditional kiss on each cheek. They shook Erdinç's hand and nodded respectfully at Kemal who remained seated, arms crossed. He remained in that position for the very brief instruction he laid down. Yes, we would give them water. However, if I or any of my family were hurt or harassed in any way, then he would arrange to have them driven out of town. Were they clear about what he had said? Yes, they were clear. He then got up and walked out the tea shop with Erdinç and I in tow.

The point I want to make clear: John Patterson and I could not build a house, live in Selçuk or, in my case, run a business without the support and backing of Kemal and Erdinç (We could join a missionary ghetto and live in our own little sin-free bubble). In return, we were expected not to do anything or behave in a manner that would bring shame on their family. We had gotten off to a bad start with them when they found out John Patterson had been funding part of the building work by offering the supporters a missionary centre. He had broken his promise and failed to keep his word.

The Kick-Ass American was not going to give up on a missionary centre and started to put pressure on the Turkish pastor and John Patterson to throw us out of the house. I also discovered that John Patterson had started a charitable trust to channel funds for The Little Farm, after he swore he would never do that. The trust was run by his wife Margaret Patterson and a friend Martin Thompson. Martin decided to visit The Little Farm to see how I was going to solve the dilemma: The Kick-Ass American versus Turkish supporters. I asked him what he was going to do if the UK Charity Commissioners found out they had been raising money under false pretences. Martin was just as surprised by my historical involvement with The Little Farm as I was by the formation of The Myrrh Trust. What became clear was his belief that it was The Myrrh Trust that was the owner of The Little Farm and I was a kind of employee. I made it clear that I had been a partner in the project from the beginning and had returned to the project on the understanding given by John Patterson that we had resumed our partnership.

Not long after Martin returned to the UK, I got a letter from him in his role as the chairman of the trustees of The Myrrh Trust. I was asked to leave The Little Farm, which was going to be signed over to the Turkish pastor's charity. John Patterson was coming out with a representative from his church to meet up with the Turkish pastor and the Kick-Ass American leader to turf me and my family out and put a Turkish couple in our place. I asked Erdinç what to do. He said he would come to the meeting but did not tell me what he was going to say. I also asked Fr. Ron Evans from the Anglican Chaplaincy in Izmir to attend the meeting. I was an active priest in Turkey and Fr. Ron was my boss.

I was on a tour in Cappadocia the week the meeting was proposed and had to take a break to attend. The meeting was weird: it started off with an outburst of abuse towards me via John Patterson. It was like he was play acting, he would never dare speak to me like that if he was on his own. The Kick-Ass American sat snarling at me hoping the Megalomaniac would strike me down at any time. After the abuse, came the instructions as to what was going to happen: a new couple would move into the house, I would move out and give them a list of monies I had spent to date, for consideration of repayment. John Patterson returned to his alter ego and said they really wanted to bless me. The house would be transferred into the Turkish pastor's charity and used by the Kick-Ass American.

What followed was an awkward silence. The Turkish pastor started fidgeting; he just wanted to get away as soon as possible with the spoils of war. Erdinç started to speak. He said John Patterson was like a brother to him and I was like a father to him, we were family. But he complained that there was no truth in this meeting, that something underhanded was going on. He said that if any action was taken to remove myself and my family from the house, then he would ensure "the Gendarme" (Army Police) would close the place indefinitely and tie it up in the law courts so it would never be used by anyone.

The Turkish pastor rose to his feet, said he didn't want to be involved in this type of situation, ruled himself out of the picture and off he went. The Kick-Ass American snarled and John Patterson asked Fr. Ron to close in prayer. Fr. Ron refused. After all the abuse, he was sure g-d wasn't interested in a last prayer. John Patterson, the Kick-Ass American and his church supporter got up to go. Erdinç and I walked them to the gate, which is the tradition. On the way, John Patterson put his arm around me saying he only wanted to bless me and my family. In that moment, his glittering image was broken. A weak man was standing before me and I grieved for the man I once knew.

After that meeting, the Turkish pastor sent John Patterson and I an email. In it, he said he would never act on our behalf again without written permission from both of us. This was a good decision. It gave John Patterson and I a chance to sort things out amicably and gave us the possibility of saving our relationship. With the reassurance that the Turkish pastor would not act against me, I decided to press on with getting The Little Farm up and running.

First things first, I needed a source of income. Hugh O'Donnell, a friend I made in Bermuda, asked me if I would find him a house to restore as an investment property. I researched the different areas in Selçuk and discovered the older, historic part of town could well be the next rising star. After looking around, I found a derelict cottage that would need a full restoration. The location was perfect, so I bought if for Hugh. When he came out to see it, he went ballistic. With full Irish charm he said, "What the feck have you done with my money?" I told him to follow me and we climbed a ladder onto the flat roof of the extension to the house. From there you have a panoramic view of the area, including the Basilica of St John, Nightingale Hill (Mother Mary's House), the Temple of Artemis (Diana) and the Isabey Mosque. Hugh is a good Catholic lad so he was in heaven on that roof. Hugh's wife Debbie took on the job of designing and fitting out the house; I was given the job of restoring it.

While looking for a site manager, my old friend Chris Haggerstone asked if I would like him to come out and help get things started at The Little Farm. He stayed five years. Chris became the site manager and our neighbour Mehmet, his labourer. This was in 2005, the days when few planning rules were enforced. It was basically down to who you knew. Erdinç was deputy head of the Chamber of Commerce and assistant chairman of the Atatürk Community; he knew everyone. His friend was the head of planning in the town and he sent the council architect to advise on the build. The roof would need to come off and a new one put in its place. We agreed to use as many of the old tiles, which were originally from France and had a honey bee motif. The walls of the main house were held together by straw and cow poo so we would have to take them down and replace them. This gave us the opportunity to extend the house by a meter. The house was in two parts. The old cottage had originally been three rooms. We made that space open-plan with a kitchen, dining space and lounge. Chris had made a beautiful A-frame roof that spanned the whole space and left the timbers exposed. Attached to the old cottage was a concrete and red brick extension. This gave us space for two en-suite bedrooms plus a bathroom for the house. Debbie O'Donnell had a great eye for detail and we included many of her ideas into the design plan.

The garden received the same attention. We built a stone patio at the side of the house and a brick open-plan kitchen/barbecue on the back wall of a neighbour's house. Debbie came over to fit the place out with Erdinç and I taking her on manic shopping sprees. Serenity Cottage was completed. Hugh O'Donnell flew in to view his investment. He stood in the house and wept with joy, then climbed the new staircase to his roof terrace and viewed his new kingdom.

Father Tarcy was the Catholic priest in charge of the community at Mother Mary's house. He was a dear man who welcomed people from every race and religion to enjoy the peace of Mary's house. He was a conspirator of unconditional love. He asked me if I could help a charity in a nearby village. They were building a centre for children and adults with special needs. They had paid the electrical contractor in advance and he had run off with their money. I took our electrical contractor over to the centre and he priced the work up. I agreed to pay for the materials and he agreed to do it all at cost. This began a long-term relationship between The Little Farm and the special needs community.

We built a relationship with a college in Swindon where my daughter worked. Her boss Andrea Howe agreed to lead a group of students to Turkey and undertake any project that the special needs centre needed doing. The following year, another teacher Carla Hitch asked if we could arrange a meeting with a local scout group. Erdinç and I visited the head teacher of a local school who agreed that Carla and students from the college could arrange a day of activities for the scout group at the school. Thanks to Andrea and Carla these visits to the special needs centre, the scouts and The Little Farm took place for several years with strong relationships built between the different groups.

With the success of Serenity Cottage, Hugh and Debbie O'Donnell wanted to continue investing in Selçuk. I had already identified other properties close to Serenity. When they knew I was interested, the local sellers put the prices up and wanted crazy money. I decided to look at other opportunities. I found an olive field in the mountains above Selçuk. It had 800 trees so income from the olives would help with the yearly maintenance. On a bright day, you could see the sea. There was planning permission for a cow shed and a dilapidated cottage on site so it would be possible to build a small house on the cottage footprint. They had a partner in this venture, Julian, a colleague of Hugh. They were hoping to build a hotel on the field in the future. They bought the field and with the change I bought them a small cottage at the foot of the hill of St. John's Basilica.

On one visit, Debbie came with me to view a field I had been asked to sell on behalf of a client. It was in the 'Valley of Reconciliation' where the legend was that two followers of Jesus were buried there. The villagers had built a mausoleum in the village to house the two bodies. There were seven parcels of land that were being sold as a single lot. All had fig trees. To my surprise, Debbie fell in love with the valley and bought the land on the spot.

Our last venture together was the biggest and the best. A piece of land became available a few minutes from Serenity Cottage. It had three derelict buildings that we planned to restore. All the rules were now being enforced and planning decisions made in the city of Izmir. It took two years to get planning permission and we were required to build new houses, two of them. We built the most beautiful stone houses to the highest specs with a small swimming pool. They were the talk of the town and we were praised by the local council for our efforts. By this time, we were building and restoring houses for other newcomers and then letting and managing their properties.

My business partner was my son Ben. He came home from uni for a break and decided to join the business. Chris Haggerstone trained him in the art of building and I taught him project management. Within five years, he was building new houses from scratch. Debbie and Hugh O'Donnell bought a majority share in our company and Erdinç joined us officially, becoming a director of the company and manager of our office in town.

At the Little Farm, we started hosting young people's groups for a period of one to twelve weeks. They were asked to live together as a community, sharing in the daily office and living a common life. We organised part-time voluntary jobs in town and they helped us to get several projects off the ground at The Little Farm. On one of these trips, Ben met Jessica Parsons and they married a couple of years later.

With Erdinç and Kemal's help, we had built a successful property investment and management company. This was a Turkish company and rooted firmly in the Selçuk community. We had a good relationship with the special needs centre who we supported and assisted in their work. The centre is one of the happiest and fun-loving places I have ever been involved with. We were organising cultural exchanges, tour groups, academic lectures and teaching young people the value of a common life. We were firmly embedded in our Turkish community, building trust and cooperation in the community between Christians and Muslims, foreigners and Turks.

Erdinç and I wanted to build more connections and I suggested to him that we work with the Selçuk Chamber of Commerce and the local council to organise a Mother Mary Festival. This would be a week of activities including a Pilgrimage for Peace, The Most Outstanding Young Woman of the Year Award, street festivals and a concert at Ephesus. We worked on this for two years. The local council promised financial support and a festival office. Local businesses promised sponsorship. The schools agreed to prepare material for the street festivals. We were ready to run, when MIT stepped in. This is the Turkish secret services. They said they would be unable to protect the participants from the militant and violent minorities an event like this would attract. We also discovered that the Catholic hierarchy were trying to scupper the event because it was Turkish led and the missionary community thought it was a "demonic" festival. I think religion is a terrible thing, so full of hatred, jealousy and malice. I am sure g-d does not approve of it. Religion should be banned.

Erdinç and I were gutted. We saw this as a big opportunity to reduce the hate and mistrust between people of different races and religions and an increase in economic activity in our region. In five years, we had achieved a lot. We had done it the Turkish way, working with the Turkish community, building trust and contributing to the social and economic welfare of our town.

Then the Obliterate (distance, diminish and delete) returned with a vengeance.

The Turkish pastor had his lawyer send me a letter in March 2010 demanding the return of *his* property. It said I had come to Turkey in 2004 and rented *his* property with the intention of buying it. I had not paid him any rent and refused to leave the property when asked. The Turkish pastor now wanted me to leave and pay him 70,000 Turkish lira in unpaid rent (the equivalent then to around £27,500). Every single word in that document was crafted into lies.

I was obviously shocked and stunned by this turn of events. Not only had the Turkish pastor gone back on his promise not to act against either John Patterson or I without our written consent, but was also lying about both his and my relationship to The Little Farm in the process. Blatant, barefaced lies with a malicious intent.

Prior to this letter, John Patterson and I had met a few times to see if we could resolve our situation. We finally agreed that the best option was for me to buy The Little Farm so he could pay back the Kick-Ass American (I had no significant money of my own but Hugh and Debbie O'Donnell had offered to lend it to me). What we were in the process of agreeing was the price to pay. John Patterson wanted more than double the amount the Kick-Ass American had raised for the house. I had offered £60,000; John Patterson wanted £120,000 (the house would be held in a charitable trust and not become my personal possession). I was still optimistic that we could reach an agreement. So, what or who had changed John Patterson's mind? The answer would lie in Northumberland, with Roy Searle and Trevor Miller, leaders of The Northumbria Community.

In May 2010, John Patterson came to Turkey to try and convince Erdinç to join him in getting Linda and I out of The Little Farm. Erdinç said he had to endure the most bitter and malicious attack on my character and reputation. John Patterson shared information about my time with the Northumbria Community that only could be obtained from the Community leaders Roy Searle and Trevor Miller. He informed Erdinç that he had met with them on two occasions, one at his request, the other at their request. He claims (to cut a long conversation short) that Roy Searle and Trevor Miller said the Community had washed its hands of me, that they were not interested in my welfare or well-being and that they would not contest a decision to force me out of the house. Furthermore, they claimed I was a financial liability, that I couldn't be trusted with financial agreements and that I had left them in serious debt. John Patterson repeatedly said, "His community said he is a liar and a thief." What on earth was I to make of all of that? Was what he said true? Had they said all of that about me? It wouldn't be long before I found out.

During the drama in Turkey, there was another equally demanding event going on in the background: The Northumbria Community Reconciliation. When we visited Hetton Hall in November 2009, Andy Raine had got it into his head that there should be a reconciliation between the Community and my family. He was very serious about the whole thing and asked Linda and I if we would contribute. Andy stated that a public apology by the Community leaders to my family and I should take place at Bradford Cathedral. This got my attention.

I had written to Roy Searle and Trevor Miller just before we left Hetton Hall in 1998. I said their behaviour in breaking their agreement and acting so badly towards my family meant I wanted nothing to do with them on a personal level. I implored them, for the sake of the future vision and vocation of the Community, to issue a public apology for breaking their agreement with us. This would put a stop to the Obliterate (distance, diminish and delete) and ensure we all had a future. They refused.

If Andy could initiate a reconciliation, then both the Community, and Linda and I would get our history back, so we agreed. Andy started down the road to reconciliation with great gusto. A friend of his encouraged him saying he had seen a picture of the Eiffel tower in Paris with a gaping hole in its middle; Andy's job was to fill that hole. He soon began to hit problems. When it came to arranging a meeting between myself, Roy Searle and Trevor Miller, Roy Searle kept dragging his feet and making excuses. Linda and I were familiar with this tactic. This went on for a couple of months. In the end, I was so angry and frustrated that I told Roy Searle and Trevor Miller that this meeting was about the future of the Community, so as the father of the Community I was coming to Northumberland. In January 2010, Linda and I flew from Turkey and stopped at our daughter Jayne's house in Swindon. I asked a friend if he would drive me up to Northumberland, a 7-hour journey. We stayed in a B&B close to Hetton Hall and drove there the next morning.

At the meeting was Andy Raine, Roy Searle, Trevor Miller, Pete Askew (a new Community leader) and myself. I hadn't been there more than 30 minutes when I realised the old record was still playing. Trevor Miller complained about the hard time he and my sister Freda had experienced in the years after I left them; they were still victims. Roy Searle wanted to know why I had come after 12 years. Andy Raine explained it was his initiative. To be honest, it was an uneventful meeting. However, I did make some interesting observations. During the breakdown in relationships in 1998, Trevor Miller was the spokesman for himself and Roy Searle. As a result, I thought he was the first cause, the instigator of the hardship that came our way. What was clear at this meeting was that Trevor Miller was playing second fiddle to Roy Searle. Roy Searle was in charge and pulling the strings. Whatever bullets Trevor Miller had fired at me, they had come from a gun Roy Searle had given him.

Andy Raine's behaviour was very odd throughout the meeting: he was nervous, anxious and was stuttering and stammering. I had never seen him like this, never. It was obvious he had no regular contact with any of these folks. When Andy did speak up, I was rather taken aback at how condescending Roy Searle was in his responses and tone. At one point, he was belittling Andy and dismissing him as if he was an idiot. My one regret is I should have popped his nose out of joint there and then. Strangely enough, Andy took it all on the chin and I don't mean the other cheek. There was no respect for Andy, no regard for who he was and how he had contributed to the Community. He too had been *distanced, diminished* and *deleted* from his role as a founder. Andy is indeed eccentric, but he is original, creative and a one-off. In contrast, Roy Searle has earned his living peddling other people's work and ideas. Like a player in a tribute band, it sounds alright but is not the real deal, only an imitation. Before I left, I asked Trevor Miller if the reason for getting rid of me was mainly financial. Caught off guard or following his conscience: "Yes," he replied, "it was financially EXPEDIENT to cut ties with you."

I was glad to leave and return to Swindon, then home to Turkey. Andy was still ringing every other day, trying to keep the contact up. I explained to him that his idea of a public apology was the only way forward.

In March 2010, we were hit with the lawyer's letter from the Turkish pastor. Andy turned out to be a great support during this time. He encouraged Roy Searle and Trevor Miller and several other leaders that knew me to contact the Turkish pastor, to remind him that they knew the history of The Little Farm and ask him to negotiate a settlement. At times, the correspondence between the pastor and our folk became almost a comic double act, with each party trying not to offend the other.

Hugh O'Donnell said he wanted to help and offered me a loan of £120,000, the amount John Patterson had asked for when we were discussing my proposal to buy The Little Farm. I was relieved, thinking this would end it. The reply was swift: they no longer wanted the money, they wanted the house and me, ruined, and out of Turkey. What's more, they had been told I could not be trusted to honour financial agreements. Who had told them that?

I contacted John Patterson myself and agreed to leave The Little Farm if he kept his word to Kemal and Erdinç. I told him we would not require any of our money back. At this point we had spent more than £80,000 on refurbishing the house to make it more user-friendly for our friends from the special needs school. Some of this money came from The Sonset Trust following the sale of The Beast and our other field. After paying off The Sonset Trust debts, we invested £17,500 in the farm. The rest came from the success of our business, our financial supporters and my personal money including Bermudan pension money. The renovation included completely gutting and refitting two downstairs bathrooms and widening the doorways for wheelchairs. We knocked four small bedrooms into two, once again widening the doorways and creating French doors opening out onto ramps into the newly landscaped rear gardens. We fitted non-slip ceramic to all the rooms in the house. We also added a new drive, paths and walls with stone stairs to the new office we had built on the hill. We built stables for the horses we planned to use with our visitors, play areas and a climbing frame for the youngsters. John Patterson had the opportunity to continue this work and build on the foundations we had put in place. Instead, he insisted on breaking his word to our Turkish family and allow the Kick-Ass Americans their missionary centre. How sad is that?!

The Turkish pastor ignored every attempt for a solution to the conflict. Instead, he had a court writ (24/05/2010) sent by his lawyer: we either left the house or went to court. Erdinç took me to see his older brother who is a lawyer. It wasn't good news: in Turkey, a "tapu" (title deeds to a property) have never been transferred to another person, even if that person has been swindled. We had a neighbour, a German, who bought a field and built a house near to us. He put the tapu (title deeds) into the name of a long-term Turkish friend. After three months in Germany, he returned to Turkey and discovered another family was living in his house. The friend had sold them the house and left with the money.

I decided to get a second opinion from another lawyer. I found one in the next town. She said the same thing as Erdinç's brother, there was no chance of winning. Gutted, I went home to pack. A couple of days later, she rang me. She had shared my story with a colleague who informed her that there was a new law known as the 'duty of a fiduciary.' She told me that a 'fiduciary' is a person who holds a legal or ethical relationship of trust with one or more parties. If we could prove this was the relationship the Turkish pastor had with myself and John Patterson, then we might win the case. After asking advice from my Turkish friends and my church authorities we were all agreed: we had to fight. My lawyer issued a writ that stated the pastor was in a fiduciary relationship with me and was now acting maliciously. Seven years later, we are still in court with no resolution.

Andy Raine, in the meantime, came back with what he said was the next step forward with the reconciliation: a public confession. He suggested that he, Trevor Miller, Roy Searle and myself would make a public confession of what we had contributed to the breach in relationships. These would take place at Easter 2010. Andy wrote that he regretted not coming out to speak to us the day we left Hetton Hall or trying to stop what was going on. I wrote that I regretted threatening to beat the shit out of Roy Searle and to take the Community to court for breaking their agreement and taking the copyright for *The Celtic Daily Prayer*. Roy Searle and Trevor Miller wrote an institutional note that said absolutely nothing.

After that event and following John Patterson meeting with Erdinç, I decided to contact Roy Searle and Trevor Miller about his claims that they had called me a thief and a liar. Trevor Miller replied to my email denying that they had called me a thief and a liar. However, he admitted he was still angry at me at the time and that both he and Roy had shared confidences with John Patterson that were unwise. One of these confidences was the fact I had left the trading company £70,000 in debt. I was angry about that because it was not true. Trevor Miller and I had worked our socks off to get the trading company back on its feet. We had called in Dominic DeSaules, a business consultant, to advise us about the ongoing viability of the trading company. Based on his advice, we had agreed to carry on, even though we would need to take a loan of £20,000. How did the company accrue a debt of £70,000? How was that my fault?

I decided to ring Trevor Miller. I discovered that the additional debt was the direct result of winding down the business AFTER I left. They had decided not to carry on even though the business was in recovery. What is worse, and I discovered this from another source, Sandra Haggerstone made them a good offer for the business that she, as the manager, built. This was generous of Sandra because she had been publicly and falsely accused of stealing £10,000 from the company. It turned out to be an accounting error resulting in a VAT payment not being logged. One of my last acts as a Community leader was to castigate the Community Council for such a blunder and demand an apology for Sandra. No one ever apologised. Sandra's real problem? She was one of my best friends. The directors turned down Sandra's offer and later, unable to find a buyer, they sold it on for peanuts.

In October 2013, there was one final meeting between myself, Andy Raine, Roy Searle, Trevor Miller and Pete Askew. I already knew what the outcome was going to be because it had been leaked to me. I still went to the meeting because I wanted to ask them about John Patterson's face-to-face so I could see their response. I knew there was not going to be a public apology because they continued to state they had done nothing wrong. They wanted me to take down my Northumbria Community website recording the history of the Community that they had deleted. They wanted a blog removed, which has been written by Linda about the "missing photographs." They claimed it put them in a bad light! If I agreed, then we could work together on The House that John Built. They were still trying to *delete* me. I asked them about their meetings with John Patterson and watched them squirm in their seats as they tried to explain why they had met with him and what they had said. The guilt was unmistakably tangible. They couldn't just leave it alone. Ten years after we had left Northumberland they were still trying to *distance*, *diminish* and *delete* us. Not only had they deleted their history now, they had deliberately sabotaged their future. It was and remains over.

Back in Turkey, another event was about to unfold which would make the court case and all the troubles at The Little Farm pale into insignificance: Erdinç was diagnosed with cancer.

We had just moved into our new office and Erdinç had joined us full-time in the company. We were looking forward to a bright future together. He had complained of having difficulty swallowing. His doctor said it was acid reflux and prescribed some medicine. It continued so he went to a specialist in a University Hospital in Izmir for tests. A week later, he got the results: he had cancer in his oesophagus, pancreas and stomach.

Erdinç was ten years younger than me. He was married to Nesrin; they were incredibly close and still in love. They had two boys Muharrem and Engin, both in their teens when he was diagnosed with cancer.

Erdinç and I had faced several crises over the years. In 2002, while working in Bermuda as a priest, I was awarded a study grant that would enable me to travel to the Island of Patmos where St. John had been imprisoned for his religious and political views. Patmos was just off the Turkish coast so I arranged to go back to Bermuda via Selçuk, and pop in and see Erdinç and Kemal. The day he was due to pick me up, my ferry was delayed. Erdinç and his business partners still decided to visit the port for a meal and a drink as planned. On the journey home, their car hit a horse that had strayed onto the road. It went through the windscreen. Erdinç and his best friend Engin were sitting on the back seat. Engin was killed; Erdinç was badly injured. The next morning when I arrived at the port and there was no Erdinç, I knew in the pit of my stomach something was wrong. He was never late. I jumped in a taxi and headed for Kemal's house. He had been trying to contact me. I was bundled into his car and we headed for the hospital. I didn't recognise Erdinç. His face was battered and his head swollen like a football. He had a broken neck. Thank g-d his spinal cord was intact. Kemal asked me to pray for him and I did. He recovered but walked around with a broken neck.

Then there was the time a friend of mine asked Erdinç where was the best place to buy a Turkish rug. Erdinç told him of a couple of places and warned him not to go to the shop at the end of the street we were standing in because it was run by dangerous criminals. My friend, thinking this was a joke went to the shop that day. He thought the guys seemed normal enough so joked that Erdinç said they were "the Mafia." They laughed with him. Later that day, when Erdinç was leaving work, they grabbed him and took him away in a car. He was blindfolded, beaten and when they took the blindfold off, he was in a cellar with several men and a gun pointed at his head. They planned to kill him. Fortunately, one of the men recognised Erdinç and told the others that killing him would be a mistake, he was a VIP in Selçuk. It still had to be resolved. Over the next three months, Erdinç and his business partners agreed to buy the factory the criminals were using as their base (it was very close to their factory). In return, the criminals would move away from Selçuk. I discovered this a year later via one of Erdinç's partners.

Then there was our crazy new foreman who threatened to kill Ben and Erdinç and who I had to let him see my dark side to get him to back off. Or the time in 2002 when Erdinç nearly went bust because of the lack of tourists because of a spate of bombs. I had a good job in Bermuda so got a loan to keep him afloat, a favour he returned when a client failed to pay their account and left us with a hefty tax bill. Erdinç paid it. Erdinç restored my confidence in people and in friendships. We had to fight and get through this cancer crisis.

The doctors suggested removing all the cancer in one operation. This would involve removing the cancer from his oesophagus and then repairing it, removing a portion of his stomach, and delicately taking the cancer out of his pancreas. It was a success: after a bout of chemotherapy, it was reported that he was in remission. The cancer could always return but there was no sign of it at present and it was not aggressive in its nature. Great! Life could get back to some normality.

Like most Turks, Erdinç worked 12 to 14 hours a day, seven days a week. He was also involved in politics and social and charitable enterprises. As a result, time for the family was limited. I chided him about this before the cancer but he wouldn't listen. The cancer was a wake-up call. He cut his working hours and quit all his commitments. We started to hang out more together as families, going for picnics or visiting new places. Life was looking good.

Then the cancer returned. This was a very different cancer, not the same as the ones before, which had not returned. It was in the liver and was extremely fast growing. A friend of Erdinç's contacted a doctor she knew in Istanbul, a cancer specialist. He explained to Erdinç that his cancer had spread over half his liver. Only an operation could halt its growth and prolong his life. Erdinç agreed and had the op. He came through it, then had to endure a very difficult recovery and more minor operations to keep the liver working. It went on for months. Linda and I were in Bermuda at the time working a three-month contract as a locum priest. We kept in touch my email and Skype.

When he was strong enough, he came home to Selçuk. We were back from Bermuda and so we started our picnics again and travelled to the places Erdinç had visited as a child. He wanted to try and get the Mother Mary Festival going again and asked me to take him to Mother Mary's house on a regular basis. He said he felt her love and presence and she made him feel stronger. Erdinç had never been an overtly religious man. Before the cancer came, he had visited Mecca to pray for Linda and I and The Little Farm. He started attending the mosque regularly and g-d began to occupy a stronger presence in his life.

The cancer spread to the remaining part of his liver. The pain increased as the liver deteriorated. I used to visit him every day and sometimes massage his feet when the pain was great. I taught him imagination exercises and he created a house by a lake. He would lie on the bed, looking out of the open door onto the lake with the sun shimmering and a gentle breeze blowing through the house. In this house, he felt safe from the bear (his pain); he could hear it in the distance but it could not hurt him. I bought him a small model boat and stuck a fisherman's prayer to the mast:"Dear g-d be good to me the sea is so wide and my boat is so small." He learned it by heart and said it when he was afraid.

Day by day, I watched my friend and brother wither away before my eyes. A bed had been made up for him in the sitting room. Family members used to come and sit around him, all silent. It was like a wake. One day, Erdinç who was very weak now, beckoned me to him, "Tell them I'm not dead yet." From then on, the TV went on, newspapers were read to him, he was included in conversations, people stopped whispering and acted normal around him. Muharrem played the guitar for his dad.

I got a phone call early one morning: Erdinç had died in his sleep. Linda and I were gutted. I went straight to his house. They had waited for me before putting him in the metal coffin. I kissed him on both cheeks and said goodbye. The Iman (Holy man) was present and invited me to join him as we said prayers together for our dear brother. Priest and Iman, sacred anarchy of unconditional love.

It is traditional in the East that a person is buried the same day. First, the body is taken to the mosque to be washed and wrapped in linen. It is then transported to the cemetery in the communal coffin and van. The funeral would take place that afternoon. Hundreds of people turned out for the service outside the mosque. Then to the cemetery for the burial. My dearest friend was dead (1/5/2014).

8. OUT OF THE SHADOWS

Psychoanalysis has had a profound influence on both my personal and professional life. It has helped me understand the human condition and what makes us tick. It helps explain the complexity of human behaviour, both personally and collectively, and our potential to do good or evil. I want to turn now to the traumas I have detailed in this book and using insights from the work of two innovators of psychoanalysis Carl Jung (1875-1961) and Jacques Lacan (1901-1981) to try and make sense of them.

Parental Abuse/Mam and Mother

We all daydream when we disconnect from our present moment and wander off somewhere else. Jung called daydreaming "dissociation" and sees it as a normal, healthy activity of the human psyche. However, there are those who have a condition called "dissociative personality disorder" where wandering off somewhere else becomes a regular feature of their lives and is part of a greater disorder.

In my story of parental abuse, I used the words "Mam" and "Mother" to describe two very distinctive personalities that shared the space in my mam's personality. She appeared to have the ability to switch from one personality to the other, while neither seemed to be aware of the existence of the other. Mother was cruel and abusive. She could verbally destroy you with a few well-chosen words, making you feel useless and rubbish at anything you did. With Mother, you were never going to amount to anything, you were destined for failure, "just like your father." Occasionally the verbal abuse would turn into physical abuse, which I think I preferred if given a choice. Mother was very matronly, commanding and dominant.

Mam, on the other hand, was maternal, gentle and protective. She was extremely hardworking and determined to provide for her kids. House-proud to the last piece of dust. However, she never felt connected to everyday things. She had a habit of daydreaming and was unable to talk about politics, religion or any "real" subject in a meaningful way. She also had an annoying habit of remembering things in an idealised way, forgetting any hardships or troubles. She could not face or listen to trauma of any kind. If something bad happened, like my dad's death, she would literally "wander off somewhere," disconnecting from her body and leaving it behind. Mam, I discovered in later life and after she was gone, had all the symptoms of Jung's dissociative personality disorder. As a result, she would not have known that Mother existed nor the abuse she gave out.

"Why do you feel sorry for the people who abuse you?" asked the psychiatrist. Well, when it comes to Mother, I don't feel sorry for her at all. She was the abusive alter ego of my mam. The last time I saw Mother was when my mam was in the final stages of dementia. She only had fleeting moments when she would recognise one of us. I was sitting on the bed holding Mam's hand when she switched to Mother. The same hatred appeared in the eyes as she screamed, "It's you! Get out of here! Get out of here now!"

Do I feel sorry for Mam? Yes, I do. Dissociative personality disorder is usually caused by severe trauma in childhood. We know Mam was sexually abused by a relative and verbally abused by my granda, who mellowed by the time we arrived. She had to work every hour g-d gave her to survive and keep a roof over our heads with an extremely painful and disabling arthritic condition. Do I love her? Yes, and miss her being around.

At the same time, I believe Mam's dark secret (trying to hide her attempt to abort me) had a profound effect on my emotional make-up. It left me with the deep and complex emotion of guilt, that it was "all my fault." An emotion that I have wrestled with for many years, in many situations, and whose power is finally beginning to wane after all these years. Do I forgive Mam? I most certainly do. She made a damming choice in the most difficult circumstances and it haunted her the rest of her life.

In a strange way, it was Mother who gave me the motivation to fight for my life, to achieve the things I thought were important and not take no for an answer. She taught me that you had to play the cards life had dealt you. As Jung puts it so well in *Memories, Dreams, Reflections* (1963): "I am not what happened to me, I am what I choose to become."

Institutional Abuse/The Church of England

NB There are some graphic sexual images in this next piece, which some people may find upsetting. They have been taken directly from the independent review (June 2017) conducted by Dame Moira Gibb DBE.

In October 2015, Bishop Peter Ball was jailed for 32 months for misconduct in public office and indecent assault after admitting the abuse of 18 young men aged between 17-25 years old. An independent review of

Ball's case found that a former Archbishop of Canterbury George Carey had colluded in concealing Peter Ball's abuse for many years. Ball had started abusing young men as early as 1977 and assaulted a boy aged 12 or 13 in 1978. Equally disturbing was the institutional violence that was carried out by Church authorities and their legal teams to silence the whistle-blowers and victims with the most malicious intent, to preserve the reputation of the Church. The report makes shameful reading.

I have heard it said many times that the Church is in a very different place now with safeguarding policies in place and the welfare of the victim now the Church's priority, not the reputation of the Institution. Sadly, that is not true.

An article in the Guardian newspaper, in October 2014, reported that the current Archbishop of York, John Sentamu, was one of five senior clergy who were informed by a clergyman that he had been repeatedly raped as a 16-year-old boy by an Anglican priest. The victim first reported the assaults in 2012 and, again, in 2013. He claims that none of the senior clergy reported the assaults to the police. Archbishop Sentamu admits he was a recipient of the information. When asked by the Guardian why the Archbishop had not told the police, a spokesperson said, "It was the original recipient who had the duty to respond, not the Archbishop." The Archbishop did send a note to the victim telling him, "Please be assured I will keep you in my prayers." The victim wanted the five senior clergy to be disciplined but as the as the offence was over a year old, the Clergy Discipline Measure 2003 could not be used and the clergy claimed it could not be applied to them.

I have heard it repeatedly from both historic and recently abused victims that the Church is more interested in protecting its reputation, concealing the abuser and shows little interest for the victim of the assault. This view is shared by people in the legal profession who have spoken to me of their frustration at the lack of transparency when speaking to people in authority in the Church of England about abuse. This was certainly my case as a whistle-blower and victim of sexual assault. It seems little has changed.

We all want to believe that sexual predatory behaviour and the abuse of children and vulnerable adults is now relegated to a darker episode in the life of the Church. My own belief is that safeguarding provisions have not eradicated predatory behaviour but merely sent it underground. I recently spoke to a gentleman who was groomed and sexually abused by a priest in the 1960s. Back then, he had been introduced to a sub-culture within the diocese where a group of priests, most married, took part in same-sex activities. They encouraged young people they had groomed to join them. The gentleman suggested this sub-culture was nationwide. In 2010, this same gentleman decided to explore ordination. Much to his surprise, he discovered that a similar sub-culture was still active in the diocese. I had no reason to question his allegations. There were times during my own work as a priest when a sexual sub-culture in a diocese or religious community would "get out of hand" and Church authorities would "close it down" albeit discreetly.

I think drastic measures are required to disrupt and dislocate entrenched cultural attitudes in the Church that enable predatory behaviour and sexual abuse to continue. To do that, we need to get some idea of what is going on and what creates the environment for predatory sexual behaviour to occur and be concealed.

Groupthink is the practice of thinking or making decisions in a group in a way that discourages individual creativity and responsibility. I discovered early on in my relationship to the Church that you had to toe the party line if you wanted to succeed. Dissent was allowed, but only within narrow perimeters and thinking outside the box was only welcome if it enhanced the Institution. What is scary is that you start adopting that posture of conformity to the point where the Church can do your believing/thinking for you. This is the reason why whistle-blowing is so traumatic because you are made to feel that you have betrayed the Church and are excluded accordingly. Because most priests are financially dependent on the Church, including their accommodation, it makes it doubly more difficult to bite the hand that feeds you.

Groupthink also fosters an air of invulnerability in an institution. Although the Church no longer has a powerful position in British society, there are still relationships and alliances with the British establishment that foster the notion of ongoing authority and privilege. It is this sense of "invulnerability" that has led to the Church "policing" itself in all matters, until recently, when pressure has been applied from external sources.

I want to go out on a limb now to put forward a theory of why the Church has created an environment where sub-cultures of sexual predatory behaviour can grow.

In Jacques Lacan's psychoanalytical theory, there are three psychoanalytical categories – neurosis, psychosis and perversion. I briefly want to look at the category of perversion and how it applies to the case of Bishop Peter Ball (as mentioned earlier). Peter Ball, with his brother

128

Michael, were founders of a religious order in the Anglican Church. Peter Ball was regarded as having a special gift to build relationships with young men aged 12-25. Many visited his religious order to receive spiritual direction from him. His victims report his abuse was sexual, violent and malicious. His abuse had a religious, erotic element to it: praying naked, sharing cold showers, performing sexual acts or submitting to intercourse as a sign of obedience and Christian love for God. It involved certain rituals such as anointing a young man's penis with holy oil to show every part of him belonged to God. While leading young men into acts they did not want to commit, he also encouraged them to acknowledge "the name of God" in these acts; they were doing it for God. This type of behaviour is consistent with how Lacan (1993, 2007) describes perversion, where for the pervert the most important is to get the victim to acknowledge the "Name-of-the-Father" (god/law).

Bishop Peter Ball has not accepted any responsibility or shown any remorse for his acts. Rather than denial, he adopted the pervert's perspective of disavowal - a refusal to see what is right in front of you; a perspective which was shared by the Church for many years.

I believe Bishop Peter Ball saw his vocation as making up for what the Church was lacking, his ability to win the trust of young men came at a time when the Church's influence was waning. I also believe he saw himself as an extension of the personality of the Church rather than a person in his own right. He saw the Church as the perfect mother and, when caught out, he expected the "mother" to continue to care for him, demanding money, favours and vindication. Sadly, this support and protection was extended to him for many years.

Of course, the Church is not the "perfect mother" as many would have us think. The only way the sub-culture of sexual predatory behaviour can start to be dismantled is for "mother" to admit her guilt and be genuinely contrite for her actions or lack of them. Unfortunately, we know that will not happen voluntarily. Therefore, another course of action is required:

1. The proposal is to make the non-reporting of sexual abuse against children and vulnerable adults a criminal offence;

2. If convicted, the institution and the individual concerned should receive significant fines and be placed on a newly instituted Register for Colluding with Sex Offenders;

3. The new law for non-reporting should be historic and applied in all

cases.

There are very good reasons to apply this new law. When a person is not reported for sexual offences, they normally continue to abuse other victims. Non-reporting is collusion. Non-reporting means victims do not get the help they need. There are those who commit suicide as was the case of one of Bishop Peter Ball's victims, others are left emotionally damaged. Not only do they suffer, but friends and family do too.

The Church, I believe, is not in denial about sexual abuse, but rather, in a state of disavowal. It refuses "to see" what is going on right under its nose. Only when the very existence of the Church is threatened, will it wake up and dismantle the culture that has persecuted the victims and whistle-blowers, whilst protecting the predators and abusers.

The Church has demonstrated repeatedly that it cannot put its own house in order and needs a firm push in the right direction. A new law, externally applied, would certainly help the process. If a non-reporting law went on the statute book tomorrow, then the five Bishops who did not report an alleged rape would be held to account for their actions. I will remember them in my prayers.

Do I feel sorry for the Church and Archdeacon Granville Gibson for their abuse and cover-up? No, I don't. Do I feel sorry for the victims of abuse by the Church and her representatives? Yes, I do.

Familiar Abuse/The Northumbria Community

In 1998, one of our friends Dave died of cancer. I had helped him and his family through this time so his wife asked me to share a few words at his funeral. When Linda, Sandra Haggerstone and I turned up at the crematorium, the place was full of Northumbria Community folk. I had no idea that the Northumbria Community leaders had been asked to speak as well as myself. When it came to my turn to speak, the atmosphere in the crematorium was charged with negativity. People folded their arms, stared at me intently and defiantly. Others looked embarrassed, perhaps guilty and avoided eye contact. It was positively toxic. At the end, as we began to leave, people turned their backs towards us, a perfectly rehearsed rejection. When we got outside, I said to Linda and Sandra, "What the hell was that about?" We were in shock. I knew every single person in that room, some I counted as dear friends; I had taken part in the joys and sorrows of their lives. I had not seen most of them for months. Yet, in a very short time, most folks had developed a hostile attitude towards us. How does that happen?

When I handed over the leadership of the Community, a turf war began. Trevor Miller and Roy Searle did not feel secure in their new position, especially as they were being challenged and jostled for the leadership of the Community by other influential people. One of their contenders was the most manipulative man I have experienced and, in this battle of wills, he frequently and, wrongly, used my name to back up his actions. As the fight got bloody, both sides looked for someone to dump all the anger, rivalry and whatever other dark feelings were spilling out. I got the lot.

Trevor Miller, Roy Searle and their rivals began scapegoating me for every problem in the Community, whether it be financial, relational, communal, spiritual, legal or practical. If there was a problem, I was the first cause. It is common practice in business for a new CEO of a company to identify problems and missed opportunities that may have been caused by the former boss. A strong and wise CEO will take responsibility for the problems and encourage his team to solve them and seize the opportunities. A poor CEO will lay all the blame on the former boss to try and cover up their own weakness. At the end of the day, laying all the responsibility or blame on the former CEO is bad for business, morale and future growth. Certainly, that is what was happening to me. Scapegoating, however, is a much bigger ball-game and it set in motion the process of *distance*, *diminish*, *delete*, which almost destroyed my family.

It is important that for scapegoating to succeed, it is encouraged by the people with the most say in a family or community. In my case, this was Roy Searle, Trevor Miller and their rivals. They all desired to be leaders of the Northumbria Community. Although I had already passed that role to Roy Searle and Trevor Miller, they felt insecure. Because they had failed to protect me when leadership was transferred to them, they recognised their opportunity, saw my vulnerability and began the onslaught. According to René Girard, it is important to "keep the secret" that is behind the scapegoating. In my case, the failure of Roy Searle, Trevor Miller and the Northumbria Community Council to honour the agreement they had made with Linda and I. Instead, they created another narrative that painted me as the bad guy.

This is when *distancing* began, by saying that we did not want to see people, thereby creating barriers between Linda and I and other people. This was to ensure that we would have no opportunity to let people know what was happening to us. *Diminish* took different forms. First, getting blamed for every problem that Roy Searle and Trevor Miller felt they had to deal with and casting suspicion over my ability as a leader. It also took the form of diminishing my contribution to the vision and vocation of the Community, which, in truth, was foundational and extensive. *Delete* is the final assault. A scapegoat cannot return to the community; it must be killed or sent far enough away, never to return. The scapegoat then becomes a spectre a ghost-like-figure in the memory of a community, carrying a dark secret that no one remembers but would cause unbelievable chaos if it ever returned.

The very worst aspect of scapegoating we experienced was at my friend's funeral, as described above. The level of hatred and toxicity was tangible from previously good-hearted friends and family. That experience has always troubled me, how quickly the mood of a group of people can become dark, leaving them capable of the most disturbing behaviour. I finally got the answer from René Girard as to why that happens. The key to scapegoating, as we have seen, is laying the blame for all a community's problems onto a vulnerable person, family or group. It then becomes apparent that the only way to save the community is to get rid of the scapegoat, at whatever cost. This gives members of a community permission to access their dark side and to do whatever it takes to get rid of the scapegoat for the sake of the community. Hurting someone for a good cause removes guilt and rewards the actions. The hardest points were when people discovered the "secret" and were then faced with a choice to confront the lie or continue in it. Without exception, people continued in the lie and as a result had to double their efforts to ensure the scapegoat did not return by turning up the hate.

Scapegoating was the vehicle by which Linda and I could be *distanced*, *diminished* and *deleted* from the Northumbria Community. I wanted to know who was driving the bus, who had run us over and whether it was deliberate.

In an earlier chapter, these are the questions I began to address:

(i) **Was our disastrous exit the result of a messy succession plan and a weakness in leadership to make decisions?**

(ii) **Was it a messy transition that created unexpected opportunities to cut all ties to me, both relationally and financially?**

(iii) **Was it a pre-planned strategy by one or more individuals within the leadership and Community Council to cut all ties**

when the moment was right?

I think we had put a pretty good succession plan into place. It was well ordered and the Community Council responded well, putting different elements of it into place. It certainly provided an infrastructure to promote anticipated growth in the Community, both numerically and relationally. During the process, there were signs of weakness in the leadership. Trevor Miller complained frequently that he was stressed and not coping. I tried to support him and address his concerns. Roy Searle's most frequent comment when faced with a difficult decision was "I don't know what to do." I encouraged him to be more proactive and prepared for decisions, making sure he was up to speed with the background of what he needed to address. He continued an old habit of deferring or delegating a decision to someone else. I do think that difficulty in making decisions slowed the process of keeping the timetable that was set out for Linda and I leaving for Turkey. However, I don't believe it was the cause of going back on the agreement made with us.

(ii)   **Was it a messy transition that created unexpected opportunities to cut all ties to me, both relationally and financially?**

I am clear now after writing this book and using diaries of the events taking place at the time that the succession plan was in no way messy. I do not believe it created the opportunity to cut ties with me. I think several other important factors were at work:

- The breach in my relationship with Norma Wise and her very public removal of personal and financial support for my family would leave us extremely vulnerable in any power play;

- A substantial grant from The Bible Society;

- After Bradford (passing on of the leadership), Roy Searle and Trevor Miller controlled the narrative between themselves and the Community Council. I believe that during this period questions were raised about my leadership skills and about the management of money (both Trevor and Roy admitted they had misled the Council, specifically regarding financial affairs). This created fear about the financial management of the Community in the future and our expansion into Europe;

- My confrontation with the trustees over the false accusation that Sandra Haggerstone had stolen money from the trading company was employed to drive a final wedge between myself and the Community Council.

It is my opinion that the factors above created an unexpected opportunity for the Community Council to cut all ties with me, both relationally and financially. This opportunity was exploited by Trevor Miller and Roy Searle to safeguard their position as Community leaders from other contenders and to ensure I had no chance to influence the Community in the future. As Trevor Miller admitted, "it was financially expedient to get rid of you."

(iii) Was it a pre-planned strategy by one or more individuals within the leadership and Community Council to cut all ties when the moment was right?

To address this question, I want to present the facts and let you, the readers, come to your own conclusions. I will be using my own and Linda's diaries that record and reflect the people, problems and opportunities we faced during the establishment of the Northumbria Community. The intention is to concentrate on my relationship with Roy Searle.

Soon after I was ousted from the Community, Roy Searle assumed the role of senior leader and Trevor Miller adopted the side-kick role. This was never meant to happen and for very good reasons. You may remember that in an earlier chapter I described the leadership model we had adopted as a community. It was based on the early Irish/Celtic monastic communities where the Abbot was the father/mother of the community, and the Bishops who oversaw mission, were overseen by the Abbot. This was in direct contrast to the European Church where the Bishops were in authority. The Irish/Celtic model demonstrated that monastery precedes mission. Mission is merely an extension of the monastic/family life. Changing the leadership model means you move the ethos away from monasticism and back to mission, from monastic community to Church Institution.

Roy Searle's second strike at the ethos of new monasticism and the Northumbria Community was to remove the tension between un-intentional and intentional. As I explained previously, a new monastic ethos is created in the tension between the two. Un-intentional is an event that forces you to your knees, it dislocates you from your former way of living. You don't choose this life, it chooses you and demands that you are fully available to it, and willing to embrace the vulnerability it will lead you into.

You can't control it, structure it or plan it. Nobody is going to throw themselves headlong into the un-intentional but if you want a new monastic ethos, you must wrestle with it.

Intentional is the opposite. As the word suggests, you choose, you decide, you control, you order, you structure. To participate in the new monastic ethos, you must live in the real tension between the two of them and be exposed full on to the un-intentional. Roy removed the tension between the un-intentional and the intentional. When that happens, the intentional assumes the lead role because it demands nothing from you. While this has led to numerical growth, it has devastated the new monastic ethos in the Community and the new monastic movement in the UK, which the Northumbria Community has significantly influenced. Missional is now the order of the day where intentional communities plan and execute strategies.

Had the Community Council kept the succession plan agreement, my new role would have been to be the Abbot General whose primary responsibility was to ensure a new monastic ethos was maintained when I was no longer physically present. I had chosen Trevor Miller as my successor because I had nurtured him in that ethos and I believed he was the best choice to maintain it and take on the role of Abbot. Roy Searle knew that I would never agree to his change of seat that put him in the place of senior leader. Nor would I have let him remove the tension between the un-intentional and the intentional because the consequences to a new monastic ethos would be catastrophic.

The only obstacle standing between Roy's desire to be head of the Community? Me.

I have already expressed the concerns I had about Roy Searle's ambition. Ambition usually has a goal. Observing Roy Searle over the years I mentored and worked with him, I identified which goals he was pursuing. First, I spotted his desire for prominence just a few weeks after he joined us. He was asked to speak at a conference and I prepared his lecture notes for him as a first step to moving him away from church and towards community. When the conference was over, I went to congratulate him for a good presentation. He was sitting chatting with someone and I sat down and joined him. The guy he was talking with was an academic and he reached over to me and asked if I would let him spend some time with Roy alone as he wanted to discuss the content of his lecture. I waited for Roy to acknowledge his sources but he stayed silent. The next day I challenged him about keeping silent and warned him of the dangers of seeking fame by association.

The second goal of Roy Searle was to be seen to be important. I had to pull him in several times over the content of his prayer support letters. Writers of prayer letters are notorious for exaggerating the extent of their work and contribution. Roy Searle was no different. As time progressed, this desire for importance became linked to his contribution to the establishment of the Community. He started calling himself a founding member and then a founder. Both Andy Raine and I made it clear to him that he was not a founder of the Community. It was not good for his spiritual welfare to make such false claims. All the essential elements from which the Community had emerged came from an earlier period from Andy, Linda and I and the Easter workshops. This is another example of seeking fame by association by taking credit for another person's contribution. If Andy, Linda and I were around it would be difficult for Roy to seek the importance he felt he deserved.

When a person wanted to join the Community, they had to undergo a series of discussions that would enable them to access "the shadow" (Jung, 1963) of their personality. Every community has a similar process because all are aware that there are elements from the shadow that can emerge very quickly and cause havoc. This was also a feature of the Community Rule, the importance of "knowing yourself."

In my many conversations with Roy Searle, it became evident that he thought he was a balanced person with few moral faults and was an overall nice guy. Jung (1963) the psychoanalyst who developed the nature and notion of the shadow, said that nice people were the most dangerous of all because they had no concept of the dark side of their personality. I like to describe the shadow as our dark side and the place where our potential to do damage to other people and ourselves is carefully hidden away. Yet, the elements in the dark side of our personality, buried deeply in our unconscious, can be transformed and become transforming when brought into the open, recognised and named for what they are: jealousy, envy, anger, hatred, lust etc.

Jung (1963) says, "whatever is rejected from the self [shadow], appears in the world as an event."

The event that we were all caught up in was *distance, diminish, delete*. The question we now must answer is who was fuelling that event and were they aware of doing that? Let's examine the evidence:

- During the succession period, I talked at length with Roy Searle about the need to protect myself and my family when we passed on the leadership. I had done this for him when gossip, innuendo and unconstructive criticism would raise its head to do damage. It's the price you pay as a leader. He never did.

- When I asked him to address the gossip from Norma Wise, Roy Searle agreed twice to speak with her. He never did.

- I think we have firmly established that there was an agreement that was made between Linda and I and the Community Council.

- We know that the leaders, trustees and other Community Council members did not honour the terms of that agreement. Roy Searle was leading that group of people at that time. He could have insisted the agreement was kept. He never did.

- Before I returned to Turkey, just before we left the Community, Roy Searle promised he would get the agreement back on track and sort it out. He never did.

- While we were in Turkey, he attempted to cut Linda and I out of The Sonset Trust. When the attempt failed, he removed all of the money from The Sonset Trust and he and two of his fellow trustees resigned. Although he denies this, a former trustee of The Sonset Trust was present when these events took place and has confirmed those decisions were made. These acts by Roy Searle left Linda, myself and the kids in Turkey with no money and no way of returning home. He effectively terminated our relationship with the Community.

- Roy Searle visited Lord Vinson to have the lease, which was in my name, transferred to the Community.

- All money paid to me by way of a salary was stopped.

- I was requested to pay rent for our house.

- Two mediators describe Roy Searle's attitude to me as "toxic."

- In 1998, Linda, myself and our children were rendered homeless and penniless.

- In 2008-9, Roy Searle had two meetings with John Patterson (at the time John Patterson had agreed the best way to solve our problems in Turkey was to sell me the Little Farm and return the money to his American supporters). Following the meetings with Roy Searle, John Patterson decided to use the Turkish pastor who held the title deeds to take us to court to be evicted from The Little Farm. Trevor Miller admits the conversations were fuelled by past anger towards me and the content of those conversations was unwise.

- John Patterson visits my friend and business partner in Turkey to get him to turn against me. Erdinç, my friend, made notes. John Patterson said he had spoken to Roy Searle and Trevor Miller on two occasions. They had described me as a thief and a liar. They had washed their hands of me. They had no responsibility for the welfare of my family. They would not oppose any actions he took against me. They had shared confidential information with John Patterson regarding my work in the Community. I was served with a court order to leave the Little Farm and pay 70,000 Turkish lira in compensation. Whatever conversations took place between Roy Searle, Trevor Miller and John Patterson, it opened the door and allowed distance, diminish and delete to enter Turkey.

Roy Searle continues to state he is a good man. If he does anything that would hurt anyone it would be unintentional, a sin of omission. He would never hurt anyone intentionally. I will leave you to decide.

Whatever conclusion you come to regarding Roy Searle, one fact is clear: the strength of the succession plan was the emphasis on continuity between myself and the Community, maintaining the essential link for the progression of The House that John built. By destroying that link, Roy Searle secured his own future but cut the Community off from the proposed growth across Europe. It took me more than ten years to get The House that John Built back on track, only for it to be de-railed when Roy Seale met with John Patterson, which resulted in me being isolated and my work being undermined in Turkey. From a human point of view, they did a very good job. There have been attempts by Roy Searle and Andy Raine to revive The House that John Built. Roy Scarle's strike on my work in Turkey via John Patterson and Andy Raine's silent complicity means they have shot themselves in the foot. My job now is to create a new ethos and language so the next generation is prepared to take on the challenge of The House that John Built.

Ideological Abuse/Missionary Community in Turkey

If I were to ask you: "what or who would you be prepared to die for?" You may get answers that jump immediately into your head such as "my kids," "my boyfriend," "my religion" or "my country." You may need a bit more time because words are not always easy to find to describe something fundamentally important to us. I want to turn that question on its head and ask you: "What or who would you be prepared to kill for?" Are answers jumping into or out of your head?

You have just taken a first step in getting the gist of what psychanalyst Jacques Lacan (1964) calls "a master signifier". Slavoj Žižek, a philosopher and psychoanalyst, gives us some idea of the relationship we have with master signifiers. He suggests that "anything a person invests their identity in is a master signifier" (Philosophy Forum, 2016). He continues, "your rationale for any major act has to do with your identity with master signifiers" (ibid). Basically, Žižek is saying that master signifiers have a profound influence on the way we live our lives and the decisions we make. Words like God, country, freedom, free market are all master signifiers that can evoke strong emotions in us. A recent example in the UK was the decision to leave the European Union. Known as "Brexit" in common speak, this master signifier can provoke strong and, sometimes, violent emotions and actions in response to it. Žižek argues that master signifiers "serve as ideological rallying positions that in the extreme one would die for" (Philosophy Forum, 2016).

The missionary community identifies with an ideological brand of Christianity. It has various names such as "bible-believing," "evangelical," "conservative" and many more. What each of these groups have in common is that they share master signifiers that encourage a violent attitude. The first master signifier is a "personal relationship with Jesus Christ"; this is crucial to their ideological conviction. People are divided into two groups: the "saved" and the "lost"; there is no in-between. The "saved" have been forgiven their sins through faith in Jesus Christ and delivered from the "wrath" (burning anger) of God and the eternal torment in the fires of Hell. The second master signifier is "a holy nation". Once you are "saved" you then become part of God's "holy nation," "His chosen people", destined for great things in the future. As a member of the "holy nation," you are in a conflict with "the world, the flesh and the devil" and must be willing to lay down your life to resist their influence. The third master signifier is "the Bible," which is regarded as God's masterplan for all of life. It must be consulted on all matters.

Once in Selçuk, I was handed a religious tract from a smiling, young man. It was the usual appeal to get "saved." I handed it back and said I wanted nothing to do with his violent ideology. As I walked away, he grabbed my arm. He had lost his smile and demanded I tell him what I meant by a violent ideology. I said the God he worshipped was a violent Megalomaniac from which he needed to be saved. He was not happy.

Whatever the tone or posture of this violent ideology and, most times, it comes across as open and friendly, its violence is lurking in the background. If you are not "saved", not part of the "holy nation," then you are "lost" and destined for hell. If that is true, you are a worthless human being and can easily be dehumanised. This was my experience, as a teenager when my family turned against me when I wouldn't play the Megalomaniac's game. It was also what fuelled the fire in Turkey.

The Kick-Ass American is on the extreme side of the Megalomaniac. He has a deep hatred for anyone who is not the same as him and he is unable to hide it beneath a friendly smile. This is the type of person who believes God will "take people out," literally kill them if they stand in the way of his plans. The Turkish pastor is also on the extreme side but can conceal it when he is pressed. This is the person who said that he would ruin me and drive me out of Turkey. John Patterson is intimidated by both men and probably regrets getting involved with them. He dug himself a hole that he could not get out of and used me to try and sort it out. I am sure it is their influence that made a sweet man turn so sour. I hope he finds himself again one day. In the meantime, the court case continues and The Little Farm stands empty. A sad affair. It used to once vibrate with life.

One of the editors of this book has asked me to show my emotions more, wondering why I haven't sounded off louder at people and in situations where I was so obviously stitched up. I think part of the answer to that is that I have had to distance myself a little and not let my emotions rule me so I could report each traumatic event with some objectivity. I want the reader to decide what the appropriate emotional response would be. However, both mine and Linda's diaries are raw with emotions, from uncontrollable anger to depression, anxiety and suicidal thoughts. I am still shocked by the size of the betrayal by the leaders of the Northumbria Community. I am also surprised at my own naivety, thinking because they were friends and family that they would never do anything to hurt me or my family. The worst thing about all of this? It has made Linda and I less trusting of people and not so comfortable being open with others.

For me, the biggest struggle has been a very serious one indeed, that is dealing with my own dark side. The Turkish pastor is a serial bully and I have had to wrestle with myself so many times to stop myself from going and sorting him out. His smugness bolstered by blatant lies reminded me of the bullies in my childhood who only responded to violence as a way of stopping their bullying. Several times, I was approached by Turkish friends who wanted to sort him out "the Turkish way." I resisted their very tempting offers. I know you can't fight hatred with hatred and though I lost my temper several times with him, I refused to physically hurt him, no matter how tempted. Unconditional love would not support it.

Each of these traumatic events, no matter how painful, opened a new episode in my life. The experience with Mother and her constant chiding motivated me to get educated so I could follow the vocation I had chosen as a priest.

The institutional abuse by the Church gave me the opportunity to rethink my religious beliefs and pursue a new type of monasticism. This gave life to the Northumbria Community, Celtic Daily Prayer and the Northumbria Community Rule, both edited and written by myself and Andy Raine. It also began the momentum for a worldwide new monastic movement.

The betrayal by the leaders of the Northumbria Community nearly finished me off, the wound was so deep. The discovery of their collusion with John Patterson to isolate me and damage what we had achieved in Turkey really says it all. Although the Community broke their promise to support me in Europe, I kept mine. I fought against illness, adversity and near death to make sure Linda and I arrived in Turkey. We built a business, worked with our special needs community, arranged cultural exchanges, built bridges, earned the trust of the Selçuk community and found faithful friends again in Erdinç and Nesrin. My roots go deep into Turkish soil and I left some of myself there. We never expected to return to the UK and our roots in Northumberland. Another chapter is about to open and the crazy thing is, I am really looking forward to it!

Following the Fire

In the middle of the darkest days in Turkey, three friends came to support us: Laura, Sheila and Anna. They spent a week with Linda weeping, wailing and praying. Whatever they were doing, it worked. The darkness that was over us lifted and we were no longer walking through mud. Before they left,

Erdinç took Anna's hands and said to her, "Here, take this fire home with you." Anna decided to pass the fire to her husband, Andy Raine, but then felt she had made a mistake. She asked Erdinç to give her more fire when she returned to the UK. The women decided to "hide the fire" in a wall around Bamburgh Castle, which is opposite Holy Island in Northumberland.

When Nesrin and the boys decided to move away from Selçuk because of the painful memories surrounding the death of Erdinç, Ben and I both felt it was time to leave Turkey. Linda and Jessica agreed. But where would we go? We thought we would look for a large house or hotel for sale near York or Durham. Linda and I were sent out as scouts with a list of properties for sale. There was nothing that we liked. We decided to go to Northumberland to see a hotel for sale, which ironically was across the road from Roy Searle. Linda and I really liked it and asked Ben, Jess and son Josef to fly over to see it. We all liked it and were keen to do a deal to buy it. However, it was priced more than it was worth and they had only been trading a couple of years. We returned to Turkey and waited for an audited set of accounts so we could make up our minds. Another hotel was put up for sale very close to the one we had looked at. Ben and I flew over to look at it. It was in poor condition.

Ben then got an alert on his phone about a property to let near Bamburgh. I wasn't keen to rent but agreed to look. It was an Edwardian hall with two further floors below the hall and a cottage attached. Six bedrooms, a massive kitchen, sitting room, dining room and large hall with a sweeping staircase. The garden is the size of a football field and well-laid out, with a lawn, fruit trees and a pond. There was the option of taking on the four-bedroom flat below us and the three-bedroom flat on the bottom floor. There are also the enviable sea views over to Holy Island. What is best about being here? Bamburgh is a few minutes away in the car and the fire that Erdinç gave to Anna rests safely in the walls of its castle. Knowing we are close to the fire Erdinç gave to Anna, warms my heart and is a powerful symbol that there is more of this story to unfold.

After the life-saving stent, I decided to look and see if there was anything else to do to help my heart issues. I found a community of doctors in the USA who had been treating cardiac patients with food. People like me, with a bypass, stents and a grim prognosis, had survived an additional 15 to 25 years and beat a premature death. It is a plant based diet without any oils, nuts, dairy, meat, fish, sugar or white flour. I have lost 20 kilos, my breathlessness and can exercise on a treadmill.

142

I now get up on a morning looking to live my life to the full, no longer as a no-hope, dead-man walking. I am currently studying to become a lead auditor in ISO 9001 2015, an international quality standard. I hope to specialise in health and social care. Ben is now fully qualified as a construction site manager, which validates his ten-year experience in Turkey.

I am working on two more books. The first, *An Introduction to Bonhoeffer's New Monasticism*, is based on a lecture series I organised in 2015 with leading members of the new monastic and radical theology communities. The second, *The dis(o)der of A New Type of Monasticism*, is where I put Bonhoeffer's new type of monasticism through the filters of radical theology and in particular the work of Prof John D. Caputo and Slavoj Žižek, with some interesting results. This book calls for active resistance to the dismantling of our welfare state and the greed that is fuelling the demolition of social democracy. I no longer identify with mainstream Christianity, preferring to stand outside with members of what I call "the non-church." I think our motto would be: "We don't believe in g-d and we are not atheists."

As for my abusers? The colour of shame is that moment when an abuser can no longer hide their secret. It comes out of the shadows and into the light. They are covered in the colour of shame. At this point, the abuser and those who have supported them have a choice: to continue in the lie or to put their hands up and admit their guilt. The latter gesture is the road to redemption for the abuser, the abused and the silent witnesses. Sadly, experience suggests, that when an abuser is cornered, they continue to pour scorn on their victim, plead their innocence and continue to claim they are the true victims.

Writing this book has been very painful for both me and my family. It has opened old wounds. At the same time, it has been cathartic, cleansing and releasing. Many victims of abuse feel guilty for what happened to them, especially when they have been surrounded by people who claim not to believe them. Those feelings increase when you are faced with false and damming accusations made against you on a regular basis, over a long period of time. I no longer have that false guilt. As both writer and reader of the book, I have been shocked at the lengths people have gone to hurt me and my family. I think the psychiatrist was right to ask me why I felt sorry for people who abused me. She was right. I did have some empathy. But not anymore. What the Church, our community, family and friends did to me and my family was malicious and deliberate.

I hope my abusers find redemption. The first step is embracing the colour of shame

Made in the USA
Columbia, SC
24 December 2017